What the Bible Doesn't Say

... and What It Does

Seven Things That May Surprise You

Second edition

James C. Bangsund

© 2017

What the Bible Doesn't Say … and What It Does:
Seven Things That May Surprise You
Second edition

Cover and layout by the author

Other books by the author:

Leaning into the Future: The Gospel According to the Old Testament
Sidelined but not Abandoned: The Fate of the Firstborn in Genesis
You Can Read Biblical Hebrew
You Can Understand the Old Testament

Edited by the author:

The Traditional Musical Instruments of Tanzania

All available on Amazon.com

To

Judy
"An excellent wife, who can find?
For her worth is far above jewels."
Proverbs 31:10

Naomi &   *Peter &*   *Sharon &*
Brian   *Christi*   *Mike*
"Behold, how good and pleasant it is
when children dwell in unity."
Psalm 133:1

Collin   *Leona*   *Fiona*
"Grandchildren are the crown of the aged."
Proverbs 17:6

Contents

Preface vii

A Note for Class Participants......................................xi

1. Adam's Rib 1

2. The Fall of Satan 9

3. Eternal Life..23

4. Jesus' Descent into Hell....................................31

5. What Happens When We Die? 41

6. What If You Get "Left Behind"? 53

7. Where Is Heaven? ... and When? 63

8. When All Is Said and Done 79

Index of Scriptures...89
Index of Subjects 91

Preface

Christ, the Cross and the Resurrection. When people tell me they are hunting for a church and ask me what's most important, I tell them first to listen for those three themes in the sermons, and then to be sure that what the pastor says is drawn not merely from his or her personal opinion (we all have many!) but rather from what the Bible says.

So why a book on what the Bible *doesn't* say?

I write as a pastor and a former seminary professor. My life has been one of teaching what the Bible *says*, not what it doesn't say; and, today, I have the privilege of serving in a congregation with many people who study the Bible seriously and, like me, continually want to learn more.

Of course, there are times when I run into misconceptions and misunderstandings – and some of those have been my own! Those which have caught me most off guard are the ones which "everyone knows" – and yet which simply aren't true. Have you ever been challenged on some point, about which you are absolutely certain, and then gone hunting in the Bible for it, only to come up empty-handed? I am always glad when those "coming up empty" moments occur in the privacy of my own study rather that in the public glare of a Bible study group!

What I also find interesting is how many of these things seem to be inter-denominational – common misconceptions that have, for countless generations, traveled "alongside" the Bible, been taught in Sunday School by legions of faithful teachers, and are found among us whether we are Baptists, Lutherans, Presbyterians, Roman Catholics or what have you.

Take Adam's "rib." Eve was made from it. Except, the actual Hebrew text says it was not a rib but something else – something that actually brings added depth to the story.

Then there is the "fall of Satan." We've all heard the story of the proud and beautiful angel, Lucifer, who organized a heavenly rebellion, only to be cast from heaven with his revolutionary minions. But you can search day and night and not find that story in the Bible – though if your search is complete it will bring you added confidence in the face of the Enemy, as we will see below.

The misconception that I find the most fruitful, exciting and challenging, has to do with our going to heaven – or not. Oh, I certainly believe in life after death, and that, because of Jesus' Cross and Resurrection, we can know of a certainty that our future will be wonderful and in the presence of God. But what does the Bible actually say about all that? There are some encouraging surprises for us when we dig in on this one.

And now, just a final word regarding matters of Genesis and Creation. In so many ways, we live in a highly polarized age. Therefore, let me say from the outset that in this book I am not going to attempt a reconciliation between those who understand the creation story as a literal scientific event and those who use words such as "myth" or "parable." I believe Genesis to be God's word to us, but I am not going to enter into the heated debate between the creationists and the evolutionists. Rather, I am going to ask both groups to check their guns at the door and sit down with me around a table at which we are going to ask a different question. That question is quite apart from – and, I contend, more important than – the contentious issue of whether the world is six thousand or 13.8 billion years old. The question is simply "What does the Bible say" about seven things. My goal is to do what is at times called a "close reading" in which we pay careful attention to the text and let it (as opposed to our personal agendas) have a voice. For me, letting the Bible speak in that way is to let God speak. Even if that is not true for you, however, I think you will find the discussions which are about to follow both interesting and informative.

What the Bible doesn't say ... and what it does. I hope you enjoy reading this book as much as I have enjoyed writing it. But, more to the point, I hope this encounter increases your joy and confidence in that which the Bible *does* say about God, about what he has done for you in Christ, and about what he now hopes for you in this present world and in the one to come.

James C. Bangsund
St Timothy's Lutheran Church
San Jose, California

Preface to the Second Edition

Since the printing of the first edition, the book has been used in several classes. Students always have helpful suggestions; this new edition contains most of them. To a great extent, the contributions consist of additional texts suggested for inclusion in the discussion and this has resulted in the addition of a number of new paragraphs. Thank you to those thoughtful individuals responsible!

In addition, the book now contains indexes of scripture references and subjects which should make it more useful to those trying to track down discussions of particular texts or issues.

A Note for Class Participants

Welcome to what I hope is an adventure with a purpose. This new edition of the book is the same as the original but has questions appropriate for class discussion added at the end of each chapter.

My goal in writing both the book, as well as providing the questions, is not merely to raise interesting points of thought and discussion – though it may have been the list of subjects such as Adam's rib and the fall of Satan that first drew you to the book. Rather, I have two goals which I hope will be met.

First, I hope that what I have written will encourage you, in your reading of the Bible, to do what is often called a "close reading." That merely means paying close attention to details that you have previously overlooked – details which may, in the end, lead you to a different and better understanding than you originally had. One way to assist in doing that is to read a Bible in an unfamiliar translation so that you hear well-known phrases in a different way. Even better, if you know another language which is not your native tongue, read the Bible in that language. In either case, whether you read a different translation or read in a different language, you will slow down and pay more attention to individual words than you might otherwise do.

My second goal is even more important, and that is to lift up that which is essential, that which is core to your being a person of faith. I first raise that issue in the opening paragraph of the Preface, above, but it will be developed more fully in the final chapter of the book.

If you are using this book in a class setting – and that is what I have in mind with this edition – then I would encourage you to read the chapter and go over the questions each week prior to coming to class. There will be a lot to absorb, far more than can be taken in simply by coming to the class and encountering the material for the first time.

In addition, by reflecting upon the questions at the end of each chapter prior to coming to the class, you will have much more to contribute to the discussion. And, as I have found out from many years of teaching, it is the questions and thoughts brought to the class by class members that really give the class legs. A writer or class leader alone can't do that.

So, let us begin. "Your mission, should you choose to accept it," is to take a moment before reading the first chapter and jot down some notes on what you have heard and what you believe about Adam's rib and the creation of Eve. Those two things, what you have heard and what you believe, may well not be the same, of course, and this, too, is important.

This assignment will continue. Each week, before attending the class, set aside some time first to jot down what you already know about the subject indicated in the chapter title and then read the chapter itself along with the questions which follow.

If everyone in your class does the same, I think you will all gain a great deal not merely from this book but also from what you each "bring to the table" when you meet.

-jcb

1. Adam's Rib
When God Takes a Side

> So the LORD God caused a deep sleep to fall upon the man, and he slept; then He took one of his ribs and closed up the flesh at that place. The LORD God fashioned into a woman the rib which He had taken from the man, and brought her to the man. The man said, "This is now bone of my bones, and flesh of my flesh; she shall be called Woman, because she was taken out of Man."
>
> Genesis 2:21-23

What the Bible Doesn't Say

We've all heard the old saw, "Woman was not taken from man's head, that she should rule over him, or from his foot, that she might be trodden upon, but rather from his side, that she might stand beside him as an equal and be loved by him."

And I can remember at one point counting my ribs after being told, by a well-meaning Sunday School teacher, that men were a rib short on one side because of God having used it to create Woman. So I checked – and was rather bemused to discover that the count came out the same on both sides! Counting my ribs today is not quite as easy as it was then, but as far as I can tell nothing has changed.

Well, today I understand why. In spite of the above quotation from the generally faithful New American Standard Bible, Genesis does not say that God used a rib when he created woman. Rather, the Hebrew word found in Genesis 2 is *tsela'* which is elsewhere translated "side" – for instance, "sides" of the ark of the covenant (Exodus 25:12,14; 37:3,5; etc.) or "sides of the tabernacle" (Exodus 26:20, 26. 27, 35; etc.), and so on. As far back as 1500 years ago, Rabbi B. R. Samuel bar Nahamani noted this in the rabbinic work *Genesis Rabbah* [1] where he said, "[God] took one of his sides, in line with this verse: `And for the second side of the tabernacle, on the north side' (Ex. 26: 20)."[2]

Side, not rib. Now *that* makes for some interesting possibilities.

... and What It Does

Most people realize that Genesis has two creation stories in chapters one and two. The first is austere in its magnificence, with God speaking into empty space and calling everything into existence. It ends with the creation of the man and the woman. The second story, which actually begins in Genesis 2:4, is more intimate and *begins* with the creation of the man (though not yet the woman) before even the plants are created. God then creates a garden and puts the man in it. So there are two stories, and they are somewhat different in their approach.

That being said, the two stories are *meant* to be read as one, and when this is done we get a fascinating progression. Chapter one gives us the creation of what can be taken as an androgynous creature, male and female combined in a single being called Man

---

[1] *Genesis Rabbah* is a rabbinic collection of reflections upon the book of Genesis for use in preaching and teaching. The date is difficult to ascertain – perhaps fifth or sixth century A.D.

[2] *Genesis Rabbah* 17.6.

('*adam* in Hebrew).[3] Strange idea? Perhaps, and you are free to discard it. But look carefully at the language (which is poetic[4]) of Genesis 1:27:

> God created man in His own image,
> in the image of God He created him;
> male and female He created them.

If the story ended there, or even at the end of chapter one, the only reasonable interpretation would be that God had created a man and a woman. But the story doesn't end there – there is yet chapter two lying before us in which the woman is created. Furthermore, the first two lines of the poetry above do leave us with the tantalizing image of God having created a single creature, with the third line then suggesting that this creature contains all the elements of male and female. I'll say more about this below.

If this single male+female creature be the case, then the "side" (as opposed to "rib") of chapter two makes even more sense. There, in Genesis 2:18, God notes that it is not good for the man to be alone and so creates a "helper" for him. That word "helper" itself – the word in Hebrew is '*ezer* – should alert us that something extraordinary is about to happen. Why? Because the Hebrew word '*ezer* is never used for one who is lesser or a servant; rather, it is most often used of God as our helper.[5]

---

[3] I am not the first to suggest this. The rabbis are already found debating it in *Genesis Rabbah* 8:1 and *Leviticus Rabbah* 12:2 (suggested dates fifth to seventh century).

[4] I'll say more about why this is poetry below.

[5] The word '*ezer* is found 21 times in the Old Testament, twice in this account of the creation of the Woman. Of the remaining 19 times, 15 refer to God as our helper.

So God causes a deep sleep to fall upon the man, and Man and Woman as *separate* entities come into existence as God "splits the *'adam*." Here is where a proper translation of that word *tsela'* comes into play.

> So the LORD God caused a deep sleep to fall upon the man, and he slept; then He took one of his *sides* and closed up the flesh at that place. The LORD God fashioned into a woman the *side* which He had taken from the man, and brought her to the man.

And the rest is history. Whether you like the idea of an androgynous creature in Genesis 1:27, or whether you consider that to be a bridge too far, the fact yet remains that the word *tsela'* in Genesis 2:21-22 really does mean "side." The woman is created from one of the man's sides not his rib.[6]

With this in mind, we need to return one last time to Genesis 1:27 – because those three lines of poetry reveal something else.

---

[6] At one point, all this led me to create a limerick based on wordplay in both English and Hebrew. Don't worry, you don't need to know Hebrew! All you need to know is two things. First, there is actually a Hebrew word, *rib*, which means not "rib" but "controversy" or "contention." That word does not appear in Genesis 1-3, but it does in my limerick.

Second, the Hebrew word for Eve, which does appear in Genesis 3, is *havah*. (And there is a third Hebrew word which you certainly already know the word *torah*.) And now, with your newly gained knowledge of Hebrew solidly in hand, you are ready for the limerick.

> There once was a *rib* on *tsela'*
> In the case of *adam* and *havah*
>   It was said to mean "rib"
>   even though there is lib-
> eral data for "side" in *torah*.

You may have noticed, when reading the Psalms, for instance, that Hebrew often says things twice using slightly different words. That's the nature of Hebrew poetry: structure, not rhyme or meter.[7] Psalm 24 is a classic example. It begins:

> The earth is the LORD's, and all it contains,
>   The world, and those who dwell in it.
> For He has founded it upon the seas
>   And established it upon the rivers.
> Who may ascend into the hill of the LORD?
>   And who may stand in His holy place?

Note how the first line is essentially repeated in the second, the third in the fourth, and so on.

In addition, in the Hebrew, each line has two parts, A and B, and sometimes those parts will get reversed in the second line. For instance, consider Isaiah 5:7 (with the A and B added for clarity):

> (A) For the vineyard of the LORD of hosts (B) is the house of Israel
>   (B) And the men of Judah (A) His delightful plant.

In this case, "the vineyard" is parallel to "plant" – both are A – and "house of Israel" and "men of Judah" are both in parallel as B. Now look again carefully at Genesis 1:27:

> (A) God created man (B) in His own image,
> (B) in the image of God (A) He created him;
> (B) male and female (A) He created them.

What do you see? The first two lines have a clear AB/BA pattern. (A) is "God created man" in the first line and "He created him" in the second. (B) is "His own image" and "in the image of God," also in the first two lines.

---

[7] For a more detailed discussion of Hebrew poetry, see my book, *You Can Understand the Old Testament*, pages 125-128.

But what about the third line? Ah, herein lies the surprise. The third line matches the BA pattern of the second, though in this case the "He created" of A expands to "them" instead of "man" or "him." But it is B that carries the freight. Again, it is structure, not rhyme or meter, that carries the message in Hebrew poetry. Twice, in lines one and two, B has been "image of God." Now, suddenly, unexpectedly, B becomes "male and female" in line three. What does it mean that "male and female" is suddenly placed in parallel to "image of God"? It means that, from the get-go, male and female are placed on the same rung of the ladder – an amazing thing in a culture that was quite strongly patriarchal.

Theology is built upon this kind of observation. Coming before the second creation story, this first statement has precedence over the "Adam-first-Eve-second" ordering of chapter 2. Whether or not you see in these chapters an androgynous beginning that leads to "splitting the *'adam*," surely Genesis 1:27 is saying that male and female *equally* reflect, and are created in, the image of God.

All of this now brings us back to that popular statement with which we began:

> Woman was not taken from man's head, that she should rule over him, or from his foot, that she might be trodden upon, but rather from his side, that she might stand beside him as an equal and be loved by him.

Perhaps that's not such a bad description, after all.

And What Do You Say? Questions for Discussion

1. Before reading this chapter, what had been your thoughts about Eve being created from Adam's rib? What are your thoughts now?

2. Do you see a difference between a literal reading and a literary or theological reading of a text? Where might this difference be helpful? Where might it be problematic?

3. A biblical "word study" considers how a particular word is used in the Bible. Why might it be important to know what Hebrew or Greek word lies behind a word we are studying? Have you discovered online tools that can help you do this? If so, share them with the group.

4. How do you understand the relationship between the two creation stories found in Genesis 1 and Genesis 2? Do you think that the suggestion of an original "androgynous" creature is helpful? Playful? A bridge too far?

5. Summarize what this chapter says about the word *'ezer* in Gen 2:18 and about the parallel structures we see in Gen 1:27. How do they begin to shape what the Bible says about the relationship of men and women? What do you believe about that relationship?

2. The Fall of Satan

Was Satan an Angel Gone Bad?

> Thus says the Lord GOD, "You had the seal of perfection, full of wisdom and perfect in beauty. You were in Eden, the garden of God …. You were the anointed cherub who covers, and I placed you there. You were on the holy mountain of God …. You were blameless in your ways from the day you were created until unrighteousness was found in you. … you sinned; therefore I have cast you as profane from the mountain of God. And I have destroyed you …. Your heart was lifted up because of your beauty; you corrupted your wisdom by reason of your splendor. I cast you to the ground."
>
> from Ezekiel 28

What the Bible Doesn't Say

If you have grown up in the church, or even if you have come to faith recently and are involved in Bible studies, you no doubt have heard about the fall of Satan; that is, how Satan started off as an angel named Lucifer who was in heaven amongst the other angels.

He was beautiful, and proud of his beauty, and at one point gathered other angels and staged a rebellion against God. God prevailed, however, and cast Lucifer and his minions from heaven to earth, so the story goes, thus eventually leading to the fateful encounter in the Garden of Eden.

But then one day you start to look for the story in the Bible, as did I, and … it's not there! It's one of those "I know it's here

9

somewhere" moments that ends with closing the Bible and a scratching one's head in bewilderment. The story is found in Christian literature and art, of course, but our question is regarding what is found in the Bible.

… and What It Does

So what *do* we find when we turn to the Bible?

New Testament

Several places in the New Testament seem to point to this event. In **Luke 10:17-18**, Jesus has just sent a group of seventy followers to go village to village:

> The seventy returned with joy, saying, "Lord, even the demons are subject to us in Your name." And He said to them, "I was watching [other translations: "I saw"] Satan fall from heaven like lightning."

This appears to fit with the story of Satan's fall. On the other hand, the verses which follow (verses 19 and 20) raise a question of "when":

> "Behold, I have given you authority to tread on serpents and scorpions, and over all the power of the enemy, and nothing will injure you. Nevertheless do not rejoice in this, that the spirits are subject to you, but rejoice that your names are recorded in heaven."

So when did Jesus see Satan fall from heaven? At the beginning of time? Or is Jesus referring to something that had just taken place [thus the NASB translation "I was watching"]? In other words, could the authority Jesus gave the seventy "over all the power of the enemy" such that "the spirits are subject to you" have

led to Jesus' "watching Satan fall from heaven" as they went
village to village? For the moment, we need to hold our judgment
as we read some more texts.

If we are left with a question of "when" in Luke 10, we are not
in **2 Peter 2:4-5**. There, just after a warning against false teachers,
we find a long paragraph which begins:

> For if God did not spare angels when they sinned, but cast
> them into hell and committed them to pits of darkness,
> reserved for judgment; and did not spare the ancient world,
> but preserved Noah, a preacher of righteousness, with seven
> others, when He brought a flood upon the world of the
> ungodly ....

Here, 2 Peter refers to angels sinning and being cast into "hell"
(the Greek here gives the New Testament's only reference to
Tartaros, a place of damnation in Greek tradition), and the mention
of Noah, which follows, suggests that Peter is referring to ancient
events. The warning in **Jude 5-6** may refer to the same event:

> Now I desire to remind you, though you know all things once
> for all, that the Lord, after saving a people out of the land of
> Egypt, subsequently destroyed those who did not believe.
> And angels who did not keep their own domain, but
> abandoned their proper abode, He has kept in eternal bonds
> under darkness for the judgment of the great day.

These references certainly fit with the story of the fall of Satan
and his angels, but they don't bring us the complete picture. For
one thing, there is no reference to Satan himself in these texts – no
mention of his being a beautiful angel, or named Lucifer, or
becoming proud and staging a rebellion. Only angels are
mentioned, and 2 Peter's mention of Noah likely indicates that
these writers are thinking of that mysterious event found in

Genesis 6:1-2 at the beginning of the story of Noah:

> Now it came about, when men began to multiply on the face of the land, and daughters were born to them, that the sons of God saw that the daughters of men were beautiful; and they took wives for themselves, whomever they chose.

Genesis refers to "the sons of God," of course – that's what's in the Hebrew – but there is a long history of interpreting this phrase to mean "angels." So 2 Peter and Jude may be referring to this incident, though we cannot be absolutely certain.

The last nine times Satan is mentioned are found in the book of Revelation. However, only those references found in chapters 12 and 20 relate to our discussion, and both emphasize Satan's character as a deceiver. In **Revelation 12:7-9**, we read:

> And there was war in heaven, Michael and his angels waging war with the dragon. The dragon and his angels waged war, and they were not strong enough, and there was no longer a place found for them in heaven. And the great dragon was thrown down, the serpent of old who is called the devil and Satan, who deceives the whole world; he was thrown down to the earth, and his angels were thrown down with him.

The mention of "the serpent of old" makes this one of only two places in the Bible that connects Satan with the snake in the Garden of Eden.[1] Verse 10, however, suggests that this war in heaven refers not to the beginning of time but to the end, since Satan is cast to earth *after* he has been accusing people: "the accuser of our brethren has been thrown down, he who accuses them before our God day and night." Likewise, verse 12 tells us that, at this point, having been cast down, Satan "has only a short

---

[1] The other is Revelation 20:2, discussed below.

time." Thus, this reference appears to be speaking of the end of time, not the beginning.

Our last New Testament text, **Revelation 20:1-3**, is the second place that may connect Satan with the snake in the Garden of Eden:

> Then I saw an angel coming down from heaven, holding the key of the abyss and a great chain in his hand. And he laid hold of the dragon, the serpent of old, who is the devil and Satan, and bound him for a thousand years; and he threw him into the abyss, and shut it and sealed it over him, so that he would not deceive the nations any longer, until the thousand years were completed; after these things he must be released for a short time.

But again, although there is a connection to the snake of Genesis 3 ("the serpent of old" can only refer to this), the laying hold of the dragon and throwing it into the abyss seems to refer to the end of time, not the beginning.

Over all, the New Testament brings us passages which at times seem to veer toward the story of the fall of Satan and his angels, but none of them give the complete story including his pride, his beauty and the name Lucifer.

So we turn to the Old Testament.

Old Testament

The first thing we note is that Satan is mentioned only three times in the Old Testament though, surprisingly, never in Genesis. Genesis 3 does tell of Adam and Eve and the snake and the tree but never says that the snake is Satan. It is not until Revelation 12:9 and 20:2, mentioned above, that this connection is made. And, although Genesis 6 brings us the mysterious story of the "sons of

God" and the "daughters of men," also above, it never mentions Satan.

The second thing we find is that there are two passages we may never have known were there that *do* sound like the fall of Satan ... and yet claim to be something else.

Let's start with the first of these two things. What *does* the Old Testament say about Satan? As already mentioned, there are only three places in the Old Testament in which Satan is mentioned (the word "devil" never appears), and as we read we get the sense that the awareness of Satan and his malevolence is a growing thing.

Job brings us the most detailed account. In Job 1 and 2, Satan poses a challenge to God, and this is what brings all the grief and suffering upon Job.[2] We may be surprised to note not only that Satan is found in heaven (!) but that he is apparently reporting back to God after "roaming about on the earth and walking around on it" (Job 1:7). Why? Because at this point he appears to be acting as God's "prosecuting attorney," wandering the earth to point out sinners. Thus, he seeks to find fault with Job – who has already been described as "blameless, upright, fearing God and turning away from evil" (Job 1:1). What's going on?

---

[2] In the very first verse of the book, Job is described as "blameless, upright, fearing God and turning away from evil." Satan claims that this is only because God has blessed him with wealth, but God says this is not so and allows Satan to remove Job's wealth, and even his family, to prove the point. To the modern reader, this seems rather poor on God's part, especially since Job is never told what is going on. But the book of Job is attacking a different issue: the standard but simplistic wisdom of the day which claimed, "If you are good, God will bless you; if you are bad God will punish you.

A clue is found in the Hebrew where the word is not "Satan" (Hebrew has no capital letters) but rather "the satan" with the definite article. (In the New Testament, it's always just "Satan," never "the satan.") In Hebrew, when it's "the satan," the phrase means "the adversary" or "the accuser" – thus my suggestion that he is, at this point, understood as the prosecuting attorney.[3]

This is also what we find in **Zechariah 3**, the second place Satan – actually, "the satan" – is found. The prophet Zechariah spoke to God's people after their return from the Babylonian exile, encouraging them to finish rebuilding the temple. At this point, one of their leaders was Joshua the high priest (different from the Joshua who followed Moses), and here the role of "the satan" as accuser or adversary is seen most clearly. The chapter begins

> Then he showed me Joshua the high priest standing before the angel of the LORD, and Satan [Hebrew, "the satan"] standing at his right hand to accuse him. The LORD said to [the] Satan, "The LORD rebuke you, [the] Satan! Indeed, the LORD who has chosen Jerusalem rebuke you!

Joshua is delivered from the accusations of "the satan," cleansed of sin and clothed in new garments – a marvelous preview of what would later be accomplished for us in Christ. The call for

---

Thus, your material status in life unerringly shows your moral status."

[3] Another point to note is that, while "the satan" certainly catches our attention immediately when we begin to read Job, he is actually not all that important to the writer of Job. Our antennas are up because we have in mind the full blown image of Satan as the enemy, found in the New Testament, but in Job he is simply mentioned to get the story, and its larger issues, launched. The fact that "the satan" is not of primary importance in Job is indicated by the fact that he is never mentioned at the end – where the reader is perhaps expecting God to turn to him and say, "I told you so."

rebuke shows that "the satan" is, at this point, seen not so much as a prosecuting attorney, working on God's behalf, but rather as one whose motives are now understood as at least suspect if not evil.

It is in **1 Chronicles 21:1** that Satan finally is clearly seen as the enemy:[4]

> Then Satan stood up against Israel and moved David to number Israel.

What was wrong with numbering Israel? Some think that David may have been doing a head count to determine how large an army he could assemble, thus trusting in the size of his army rather than trusting in God. Be that as it may, what stands out here is that this is the first and only time that we encounter *satan* with no definite article in the Old Testament – that is, Satan and not "the satan." And here he is clearly understood as the enemy of God's people.

So these are the three places where Satan is mentioned in the Old Testament – Job, Zechariah and 1 Chronicles. Yet none of them come close to describing the "fall of Satan."

So where, then, is that story found?

There are two more rather obscure passages we have not yet considered. Neither of them mentions Satan, yet both are highly suggestive. The first is **Isaiah 14:12-15**, the Latin translation[5] of

---

[4] The relationship between this text and (the earlier) 2 Samuel 24 is important but complicated and cannot be dealt with here.

[5] This Latin version of the Bible is known as the Vulgate, translated by Jerome in the late fourth century. It will become important again when we get to the chapter on Jesus' "descent into hell" and when we discuss "paradise."

which refers to Lucifer:

> How you have fallen from heaven, O star of the morning
> [Latin: Lucifer], son of the dawn! You have been cut down to
> the earth, you who have weakened the nations! But you said
> in your heart, "I will ascend to heaven; I will raise my throne
> above the stars of God, and I will sit on the mount of
> assembly in the recesses of the north. I will ascend above the
> heights of the clouds; I will make myself like the Most High."
> Nevertheless you will be thrust down to Sheol, to the
> recesses of the pit.

The second passage is the one with which our chapter opened:

> Thus says the Lord GOD, "You had the seal of perfection, full
> of wisdom and perfect in beauty. You were in Eden, the
> garden of God …. You were the anointed cherub who covers,
> and I placed you there. You were on the holy mountain of
> God …. You were blameless in your ways from the day you
> were created until unrighteousness was found in you. … you
> sinned; therefore I have cast you as profane from the
> mountain of God. And I have destroyed you …. Your heart
> was lifted up because of your beauty; you corrupted your
> wisdom by reason of your splendor. I cast you to the
> ground."

That's from **Ezekiel 28:12-17**, and you may have noted that
several phrases have been dropped out. Such omissions should
generally make you suspicious, although most of the missing words
just describe various precious stones making up the covering of the
one being denounced by God.

Two of the phrases that were dropped, however, are
significant. In verse 16, we read, "By the abundance of your trade
you were internally filled with violence." Satan is never associated
with trade, of course. But it is the opening verses of the chapter

which bring the clarifying surprise:

> The word of the LORD came again to me, saying, "Son of man, say to the leader of Tyre …."

Ezekiel 28, it turns out, is not speaking of Satan but is rather a prophecy against the prince of Tyre, a trade city to the north of Israel. Likewise, the prophecy of Isaiah 14 against one called Lucifer, above, begins with the words, "You will take up this taunt against the king of Babylon."

So these two texts, which have language that is so clearly evocative of the "fall of Satan" story, turn out to refer instead to earthly rulers. Where does that, then, leave us? The answer lies with two final, but external, influences we haven't yet considered.

Two Outside Influences

The first influence comes from a book that, while influential, didn't make it into the Bible: the book of Enoch[6] in which the "sons of God" of the Genesis 6 account (above) are called "angels" and even given names. In Enoch 10, because of the sin of these "angels," God tells the archangel Michael to

---

[6] Who was Enoch? Two men named Enoch are mentioned in Genesis, the first the son of Cain and the other a fifth generation descendant of Seth, the third son of Adam and Eve. This second Enoch is described as a very faithful man who, in Genesis 5:24, "walked with God; and he was not, for God took him." The intriguing idea of God taking someone directly to be with him led to much speculation on the part of later writers – for instance, what if Enoch came back and reported on what he had seen? So it was that a later writer, around 300 B.C. after the close of the Old Testament period, produced the book of Enoch to provide just such a "report."

bind them fast for seventy generations in the valleys of the earth, till the day of their judgement and of their consummation, till the judgement that is for ever and ever is consummated. In those days they shall be led off to the abyss of fire: and to the torment and the prison in which they shall be confined forever.

So here we have our "fallen angels."

It was a second influence, however, that has really been the greatest. In 1667, John Milton wrote *Paradise Lost,* and it is in this book that we find the popular story of the "fall of Satan" with all of its details. In the opening chapter of the book, Milton pulls together the pieces we have noted above and writes of Satan:

He trusted to have equal'd the most High,
If he oppos'd; and with ambitious aim
Against the Throne and Monarchy of God
Rais'd impious War in Heav'n and Battel proud
With vain attempt. Him the Almighty Power
Hurld headlong flaming from th' Ethereal Skie
With hideous ruine and combustion down
To bottomless perdition, there to dwell
In Adamantine Chains and penal Fire,
Who durst defie th' Omnipotent to Arms.

Milton's telling provides much more detail but the above excerpt gives the general idea.

When All is Said and Done

Having now looked at all the passages in the Bible that might relate to the fall of Satan, along with some outside material, what can we say? The first thing is that the classic story, with all its parts, is simply not found in the Bible. Rather, it is something that has been handed down from generation to generation outside of – or perhaps we might say alongside – the Bible, influenced by the book of Enoch and, to an even greater extent, by Milton's *Paradise Lost*.

Having said this, of course, one is still left wondering, "Where *did* Satan come from?" Two thoughts come to mind, the first one purely speculative. Certainly, the language in the texts from Isaiah and Ezekiel is highly suggestive and seems to go far beyond anything that could be said of mere earthly rulers. What, after all, is being suggested in phrases such as "How you have fallen from heaven," "I will make myself like the Most High," "You were in Eden, the garden of God," and "your heart was lifted up because of your beauty"? Are we supposed to see in these texts a hint of something that, ultimately, is beyond our understanding? Different people will no doubt come to different conclusions on the matter at this point.

The second though, though, is of greater importance. We need to understand that Satan is not a god and is not "equal but opposite" to God. Note this in particular: the Bible nowhere suggests that Satan is omniscient, omnipotent or omnipresent. Rather – and this, too, is of critical importance – the Bible describes Satan as a "creature," that is, as finite and a part of God's creation.

How do we know this? We see this when Revelation 12:9 and 20:2 connect Satan with "the serpent of old," which no doubt means the snake in Genesis 3. Genesis 3, in turn, opens with the words "Now the serpent was more crafty than any beast [Hebrew, "living thing"] of the field which the LORD God had made." The implication here is that the serpent (and thus, through the Revelation connection, Satan) is something which "God had made,"[7] a "creature," a created being. (Even the passage we considered from Ezekiel 28 mentions "the day you were created.") The question of why God would do this remains a mystery, but one thing is clear: Satan must ultimately bow to God and is, therefore, not a threat to the believer.

In short, whatever conclusions we finally draw regarding the fall of Satan, we can be clear about the most important thing: Satan is not a god, does not have the power of God, and, in Christ, is already a defeated enemy. A follower of Christ will take him seriously but has absolutely no need to fear him. The "serpent of old" was defanged by the Cross and Resurrection.

And What Do You Say? Questions for Discussion

1. Had you heard the story of the fall of Satan? If so, when and where did you first hear it?

2. We see that the story, as most of us have heard it, is not found in straightforward form in the Bible. It appears to have been assembled from disparate pieces of scripture. Why do you think this was done?

3. What do you think most people think about the relationship of God and Satan? That they are equal but opposite? That they are both divine (that both are gods)? That both are omniscient,

---

[7] Thus the RSV's "more subtle than any *other* wild creature that the Lord God had made."

omnipotent and omnipresent? What does the Bible say?

4. How is the answer to the previous question affected when we realize the Bible describes Satan as a "creature"?

5. Is there a reason to fear Satan? Do you fear Satan? What is the proper attitude of the Christian toward Satan?

3. Eternal Life
Did Adam and Eve Lose Their Immortality?

> She says the snake advises her to try the fruit of the tree, and says the result will be a great and fine and noble education. I told her there would be another result, too – it would introduce death into the world. That was a mistake – it had been better to keep the remark to myself; it only gave her an idea …. I advised her to keep away from the tree. She said she wouldn't. I foresee trouble. Will emigrate.
> *Extracts from Adam's Diary* by Mark Twain[1]

But he didn't emigrate; rather, he stayed around long enough to get evicted. But die? Here we have a puzzle. In Genesis 2:17, God had said, "from the tree of the knowledge of good and evil you shall not eat, for in the day that you eat from it you will surely die." Yet, as the snake had said, no one died "in the day that" they ate from the tree.[2]

The snake. His flickering forked tongue had not only announced that that they would not die but had said that they would become "like God, knowing good and evil." Turns out the snake didn't lie (more on this point in a moment). What are we to

---

[1] This delightful work has been combined with *Eve's Diary* and four other connected pieces in a single book, *The Diaries of Adam and Eve: Translated by Mark Twain*, Don Roberts, ed., San Francisco: Fair Oaks Press, 1997.

[2] Note, by the way, that Genesis never mentions an apple! The apple appears in European traditions, perhaps because of confusion between two very similar Latin words meaning *evil* and *apple*.

make of that?

What the Bible Doesn't Say

It may surprise you to discover that Genesis doesn't say that Adam and Eve lost their immortality because of sin. Here's how that plays out.

Genesis 1 and 2 bring us creation. Everything God creates is declared good, and the high point of God's activity is the creation of the man and the woman. On the way to completing his creation, God plants a garden in Eden, and then, in Genesis 2:9, we read:

> Out of the ground the LORD God caused to grow every tree that is pleasing to the sight and good for food; the tree of life also in the midst of the garden, and the tree of the knowledge of good and evil.

We sometimes forget that there were *two* trees of note in the garden: not merely the "tree of the knowledge of good and evil" but also "the tree of life in the midst of the garden." The latter is important enough that its location is specified: "in the midst of the garden." The location of the tree of the knowledge of good and evil is not mentioned, perhaps because Adam didn't need to know; it was off limits; they weren't supposed to go there.

Five verses after God announces "in the day that you eat from it you will surely die" (Genesis 2:17), Eve is created. Six more verses and the snake is saying "You surely will not die" (or "You will not certainly die," NIV). And they don't. At least not for a long time. Eve's death is not recorded, and Adam, we are told, lived nine hundred and thirty years (Genesis 5:5).

So they didn't live forever. But the question remains: Were they immortal creatures – creatures possessed of eternal life – before they ate of the forbidden fruit?

… and What It Does

As I already mentioned, the snake does not lie. That being said, the snake was still not to be trusted. He tells the truth, but not the whole truth.

The serpent said to the woman, "You surely will not die! "For God knows that in the day you eat from it your eyes will be opened, and you will be like God, knowing good and evil."

That's Genesis 3:4-5, and by Genesis 3:22 God notes:

> "Behold, the man has become like one of Us, knowing good and evil …."

So the snake does not lie. But you'll note that my quotation of Genesis 3:22, above, ends with four dots – suggesting that there is more to come. And indeed there is. The complete quotation, which runs to the end of Genesis 3, is as follows:

> Then the LORD God said, "Behold, the man has become like one of Us, knowing good and evil; and now, he might stretch out his hand, and take also from the tree of life, and eat, and live forever"— therefore the LORD God sent him out from the garden of Eden, to cultivate the ground from which he was taken. So He drove the man out; and at the east of the garden of Eden He stationed the cherubim and the flaming sword which turned every direction to guard the way to the tree of life.

So they were driven out of the garden[3] – but did they lose their

---

[3] By the way, if you are a careful reader, you will note an important side

immortality as a result of all of this? The answer is No … because they never had it to begin with! Read verse22 again carefully:

> Then the LORD God said, "Behold, the man has become like one of Us, knowing good and evil; and now, he might stretch out his hand, and take also from the tree of life, and eat, and live forever"—

The Hebrew actually says, "And now, *lest* he stretch out his hand …." Ah, yes. That tree of life. We had almost forgotten about it. The tree they never got to. It had been there providing the *potential* of immortality – had they gone to it, they apparently would have become immortal. I say "apparently" because now we'll never know for sure.[4] Instead of going to the tree of life,

---

issue here: only Adam ("the man") appears to get driven out of the garden. Now we shouldn't make too much of this; as soon as we move into chapter 4, we learn that Eve goes with him. But this initial statement that God "drove the ***man*** out" (emphasis added) may suggest that we shouldn't be too quick to put all the blame for this downfall upon Eve. Indeed, it's often overlooked that Eve was not alone in that fateful encounter:

> When the woman saw that the tree was good for food, and that it was a delight to the eyes, and that the tree was desirable to make one wise, she took from its fruit and ate; and she gave also to her husband ***with her*** (emphasis added), and he ate.

So, while Eve at least tried to argue with the snake, Adam appears to have been standing right there beside her, dumb as a post, saying nothing.

[4] Of course this is not the end of the matter. The tree of life makes a reappearance in the very final chapter of the Bible, in Revelation 22:2. There, in the center of the "new Jerusalem coming down out of heaven," "in the middle of its street," a river flows; and

> on either side of the river was the tree of life, bearing twelve kinds of fruit, yielding its fruit every month; and the leaves of the tree were for the healing of the nations.

Although the tree lies "on either side of the river," it is singular – *the*

which was available to them, they instead went after the other tree – the forbidden tree – seeking to "become like God, knowing good and evil."

So there you have it.

But one final question remains, and it used to trouble me. Why was the tree forbidden? Isn't it good – even necessary – to know the difference between good and evil? Why was God holding out on us? That troubling thought was put into play by the snake when he told Adam and Eve, "God knows that in the day you eat from it your eyes will be opened, and you will be like God, knowing good and evil."

"God knows," the snake hissed. Well, the text doesn't say that he hissed, but he was certainly sowing seeds of doubt and suspicion. "God doesn't want you to be like him. God is holding out on you. Just taste and you will see."

But what then happened? The truth but not the whole truth. God conceded that they – and we – became "like God, knowing good and evil." But it was a sad concession, because God knew, as they did not, what would then follow.

Read the rest of Genesis – the stories of Cain and Abel, of Sarah and Hagar, of Jacob and Esau, of Jacob and Laban, of Joseph and his brothers – and you will see. You will read of a series of dysfunctional families in which people know the good but do the evil – in which people play God with the lives of others.

---

tree of life – clearly linking it to the original tree in the garden which had been lost to humanity. And its leaves provide the healing so long needed by all.

What this all means becomes clear when we come to the end of Genesis with Joseph's brothers trembling before him. Finally, someone has actually "become like God" – or at least come close. Joseph has become number two man in Egypt, second only to Pharaoh himself, and he is perfectly positioned to take vengeance on his brothers.[5]

And what does he say? We want to pay attention, since this is the final speech in Genesis, and the point of a book is often found at its end. Joseph, towering over his groveling brothers, looks down on them and, instead of snarling "Off with their heads," says:

> "Fear not, for am I in the place of God? As for you, you meant evil against me; but God meant it for good, to bring it about that many people should be kept alive, as they are today. So do not fear; I will provide for you and your little ones." Thus he reassured them and comforted them.
>
> Genesis 50:19-21

"Fear not." That's God language. "Am I in the place of God?" Ah, that is the question, is it not? Throughout Genesis, beginning with the Adam and Eve and the forbidden tree, people have been seeking to put themselves in the place of God – seeking to play God with the lives of others. And I can imagine Joseph's cowering brothers thinking to themselves, "Well, now, that's a mighty interesting question you ask, brother Joseph. Because at this particular juncture – at this particular moment in our lives – you are very much 'in the place of God.' A snap of your fingers, and ...."

But Joseph continues. "You meant evil against me, but God

---

[5] If you are unfamiliar with the gripping story of Joseph and his brothers, be sure to read Genesis 37-50.

meant it for good." And there it is. He names it. Yes, we have "become like God" knowing good and evil. But, knowing the good, we do the evil. *Only God, and God alone, both knows and does the good.*

So what happened, back when the forbidden fruit was taken? Let me suggest this: we gained a knowledge that was beyond our ability to use or control – a knowledge that exceeded our design specs, as it were. By forbidding access to the tree of the knowledge of good and evil, God was not holding out on us; rather, he was seeking to protect us – to protect us from a weight of knowledge we could not bear.

And, once that unbearable knowledge had been grasped, the only thing that would make things worse would be if those who now knew the good but did the evil were to live forever. In the words of Mark Twain's Adam, "I foresee trouble."

So was death a mercy, after all?

And What Do You Say? Questions for Discussion

1. Although Genesis never says that the snake in the garden is Satan, the book of Revelation makes that connection and the snake is clearly not on the side of either God or people. In what sense does the snake tell the truth but not the whole truth?

2. When the man and the woman take of the forbidden fruit, God responds by cursing the snake and the ground – but not the man and the woman. Yet there are consequences. What are they? Is it wrong to use our creative abilities to offset those conse-

quences (for instance, relieving the pain of childbirth or using machines to farm)? Why or why not?

3. What is wrong with knowing good and evil? Could we be fully human without this knowledge?

4. What do you think of the speculative suggestion that such knowledge may have "exceeded our design specs" or been an "unbearable knowledge"?

5. The final question of the chapter suggests that death may have been "a mercy." How could that be so? And how is death also not the last word?

4. Jesus' Descent into Hell

What Is the Apostles' Creed Talking About?

I believe in God, the Father almighty, creator of heaven and earth.

I believe in Jesus Christ, his only Son, our Lord. He was conceived by the power of the Holy Spirit and born of the Virgin Mary. He suffered under Pontius Pilate, was crucified, died, and was buried. **He descended into hell.** On the third day he rose again. He ascended into heaven, and is seated at the right hand of the Father. He will come again to judge the living and the dead.

I believe in the Holy Spirit, the holy Christian Church, the communion of saints, the forgiveness of sins, the resurrection of the body, and the life everlasting. Amen.

The Apostles' Creed

Every Sunday, throughout the world, Christians unite in worship and, in many congregations, express their faith by confessing together the ancient words of the Apostles' Creed. Although it's not likely that this creed was actually written by the Apostles, it is certainly ancient and represents the *faith* of the Apostles.

It was originally written in Latin, and is first mentioned in a letter from an early church leader in the year 390 AD. When we use it, we not only give the world a concise statement of what we believe but we also take our stand alongside brothers and sisters in Christ throughout the world as well as down through the centuries.

Perhaps you have used it in worship. And perhaps you, like I, have wondered just what is meant by the short sentence, right in the middle, that says "He (that is, Jesus Christ, the Son of God) descended into hell."[1]

Every other phrase is pretty straightforward: creation; virgin birth; trial, crucifixion and resurrection; Christ's return at the end of the age; the Holy Spirit; the Church; and the hope in which we live and in which we one day will die. We can point to passages from the Bible to support all of these things. But what about Jesus' "descent into hell"?

As a child, I had odd images in my mind – sort of a negative Ascension. Instead of Jesus going up into the clouds, I envisioned him descending into a smoky pit that went all the way down to fiery caverns occupied by Satan and those who were lost.

But why? Hadn't he already suffered on the cross and died? Wasn't that enough? And did he suffer in hell?

What the Bible Doesn't Say

Let's cut to the chase. The Bible doesn't actually say that Jesus descended into hell; but it does say some interesting things that have led to this phrase in the Apostles' Creed. Perhaps, if you use this confession in worship, you say "he descended to the dead." Or you may have seen worship books in which the words "into hell" have a footnote or asterisk leading to the words "to the dead." That alternate reading is our clue that there are some things at play here.

---

[1] There are traditions which skip this phrase – not simply because they don't like it but because some early versions of the Apostles' Creed do not include it. We will not be entering into that discussion here.

We need to begin with the word "hell." It's an English word, of course, but Jesus and the disciples spoke Aramaic and then everything in the New Testament was translated into, and written in, Greek. So we've got to do a little digging to find just what was said in the first place.

There are several words which appear in the Bible: hell, Sheol, the pit, Hades ... even the lake of fire at the end of Revelation which swallows up all of the preceding along with death itself.

These words do not all mean the same thing. Sheol is found in the Old Testament and Hades in the New. Neither word means "hell;" both refer to a traditional place of the dead where, it was believed, all people eventually go, good, bad or indifferent. The reason Sheol (and "the pit," which means the same thing) is feared in the Old Testament is not because it is a place of suffering but rather because it was understood to be away from God. The Psalmist even uses that point in Psalm 30:9 to bargain with God, reasoning that, if he dies, God will no longer hear his praises:

> "What profit is there in my blood, if I go down to the pit? Will the dust praise You? Will it declare Your faithfulness?

Hell, on the other hand, is not found in the Old Testament, and in the New Testament it is the English translation of a single Greek word, *gehenna*. This unusual Greek word appears a dozen times in the New Testament and is used primarily by Jesus in Matthew (seven times), Mark (three times), and in Luke (once). James 3:6 gives us the remaining occurrence.[2]

---

[2] Another word for "hell," a form of the Greek word *tartaros*, appears once in 2 Peter 2:4 and refers to the Greek place of the damned. It was mentioned in the earlier chapter on the "fall of Satan."

So what is *gehenna*? *Gehenna* is simply a Greek attempt to pronounce the Hebrew words *gey hinnom*, or Valley of Hinnom, a valley located just southwest of Jerusalem. Early on, it had been the location of child sacrifice, a practice so abhorred that in the seventh century BC King Josiah defiled the place, scattering it with bones, carcasses and other filth. As a result, it eventually became, in effect, a cesspit and dump for the city of Jerusalem.

It is for this reason that, when Jesus wanted a word to describe the awful end of those who died apart from God, he used the word *gehenna*. And it is that word that gets translated "hell" in today's English language New Testaments.

So now, with all this data, what is being said in the Apostles' Creed? This ancient confession of faith was originally penned in Latin, and the phrase "descended into hell" is thus found as "descendit ad inferos." So what is *inferos*? The easiest way to answer that question is to see how it is used in the Vulgate, Jerome's 4th century Latin translation of the Bible. And in the Vulgate, *inferos* is used only to translate Sheol in the Old Testament and Hades in the New – both words meaning the traditional place of the dead, where all people go, good, bad or indifferent. The New Testament word *gehenna* – the word translated "hell" in English translations – is simply left as it is and written as *gehenna* in the Vulgate. So it appears that what the Apostles' Creed is saying is that Jesus descended not "into hell" but "to the dead." Thus, the alternate reading found in some worship books is actually the correct reading.

But what does this *mean*? Why would Jesus "descend to the dead" between his crucifixion and resurrection?

... and What It Does

Here, finally, we get to what the Bible has to say about all this – but it's going to take a bit of jumping around. I give you that *caveat* because, normally, a writer who jumps around a lot from text to text is not to be trusted. Such activity usually represents "proof texting," the careful selecting of unrelated verses (often in varying translations) which just happen to support the writer's argument. (This is similar to grabbing a single sentence from the Sports page, one from the metro section, another from an editorial, then slapping them together in a way that constructs a meaning foreign to all of them and saying, "The New York Times says ....")

In this case, however, the Bible says very little about our subject and so we have no choice except to look at four separate texts from Matthew, John, Ephesians and 1 Peter.

Now, as I've already mentioned, the Bible nowhere says that Jesus descended into hell, but in several places it does give images of him descending – on a mission – to the realm of the dead.

Jesus himself may suggest this in **Matthew 12:40**. There he responds to a request for a sign from group of scribes and Pharisees by giving them the "sign of Jonah":

> for just as Jonah was three days and three nights in the belly of the sea monster, so will the Son of Man be three days and three nights in the heart of the earth.

The "three days and three nights" is figurative, of course – Friday afternoon to Sunday morning covers less than 48 hours (though this period involves *parts* of three separate days). And the "heart of the earth" may simply refer to burial. In **John 5:25**, however, Jesus says something that pushes things beyond that:

> Truly, truly, I say to you, an hour is coming and now is, when the dead will hear the voice of the Son of God, and those who hear will live.

Should we connect this reference to "the dead" hearing his voice to his time "in the heart of the earth"?

To answer that question, we need to move from the Gospels to the Letters. In **Ephesians 4**, we find a discussion of our being given grace "according to the measure of Christ's gift." In verses 8-10, this reference to "gift" leads the writer to quote Psalm 68, a psalm in which he sees God's victory having future implications with respect to Jesus. He writes:

> Therefore it says [in Psalm 68:18], "When he ascended on high, he led captive a host of captives, and he gave gifts to men." Now this *expression*,[3] "He ascended," what does it mean except that He also had descended into the lower parts of the earth? He who descended is Himself also He who ascended far above all the heavens, so that He might fill all things.

What was the purpose of this descent "into the lower parts of the earth"? In our fourth text, **1 Peter 3:18-20**, we read:

> For Christ also died for sins once for all, *the* just for *the* unjust, so that He might bring us to God, having been put to death in the flesh, but made alive in the spirit; in which also He went and made proclamation to the spirits *now*[4] in

---

[3] The word has been italicized in the New American Standard Bible (NASB), from which this quote is taken, to show that it has been added by the editors. It does not appear in the Greek.

[4] Again, the italicized word "now" has been added in the NASB. It is not found in the Greek and other translations do not include it.

prison, who once were disobedient, when the patience of God kept waiting in the days of Noah, during the construction of the ark, in which a few, that is, eight persons, were brought safely through *the* water.

A few verses later, in **1 Peter 4:6**, we read:

For the gospel has for this purpose been preached even to those who are dead, that though they are judged in the flesh as men, they may live in the spirit according to *the will of* God.

So there you have it. These are the verses which speak of Jesus' descent. They speak of this event occurring between his death and resurrection and they describe it as being "in the heart of the earth" so that "the dead will hear the voice of the Son of God" in order that, though they died sinners, "they may live in the spirit."

From all of this – beginning with our original discussion of the words that appear in the Bible and in the Apostles' Creed and continuing through our exploring of what various verses of the Bible actually say – it appears that the Bible is hinting at a descent not to hell but rather to the place of the dead, known in the Old Testament as Sheol and in the New Testament as Hades and understood to be somewhere deep in the earth. Thus, the Apostles' Creed – in its original Latin, not in our modern English translations – uses the word *inferos* which, in the Vulgate, points to this "place of the dead" and not to *gehenna*, the word for hell.

The basis for this confession is found in the New Testament texts which we have just looked at. In them, the purpose of Jesus' "descent" is given to be the proclamation of salvation to those in ancient times (the days of Noah are mentioned).

The question, of course, is what to make of it. We have a

sense of what heaven and hell are about but not of a general place where all the dead go. (Purgatory is another issue altogether and is pretty much confined to Roman Catholics.)

With so few verses, we aren't going to be able to arrive at a definitive answer here. Major doctrines are not to be based upon small numbers of references in scripture, and I must confess that, were I to have been on the committee formulating the Apostles' Creed, I might have raised the question, "Is this particular matter one of such unquestionable and important standing that we want to include it alongside die-for matters such as the Crucifixion and Resurrection?"

But I think we *can* tease out the major concern here. We who have faith in Christ are saved by God's grace through that faith because of Christ's suffering, death and resurrection. But what about those who lived *before* the time of Christ? What about, say, the grandparents and great grandparents of Peter, James and John? Even if they were faithful Jews who did their best to keep the Jewish law, perform sacrifices, and make trips to the temple, they never heard the name of Jesus and never had a *chance* to believe in him.

Although we may not be able to explain completely what the above verses from Matthew, John, Ephesians and 1 Peter bring to us, one thing seems clear: they are telling us that God was just as concerned for those who lived before the time of Jesus as he was for the disciples and those who lived after them, including you and me. And it is that conviction that is found embedded in both scripture as well as the Apostles' Creed – the conviction that God's concern and his salvation reached "backward" from the cross to Isaiah, David, the sons of Israel, Jacob, Abraham, and even to those in the age of Noah, just as much as it reaches forward to you and to me.

That's the nature of God – this God whom we worship and "who wants all people to be saved and to come to a knowledge of the truth" (1 Timothy 2:4). And, when the Apostles' Creed is translated correctly, that's what it is confessing.

And What Do You Say? Questions for Discussion

1. If you are familiar with the Apostles' Creed, what has been your understanding of Jesus' "descent into Hell"?

2. What is the difference between Hell and Hades? Where do the biblical images of Sheol and Gehenna fit?

3. What seems to be the concern of the passages quoted from John, Ephesians and 1 Peter?

4. After reading the chapter, how do you now understand what is being confessed in the Apostles' Creed regarding Jesus "descending into Hell"?

5. Looking at the large picture: What, in general, is being said about God in the quoted Biblical texts and, thus, in the Apostles' Creed?

5. What Happens When We Die?
The Problem with Immortal Souls and Angels

> We look for the resurrection of the dead, and the life of the world to come.
>
> From The Nicene Creed[1]

"Though our little son is no longer with us, we know he is an angel looking down on us from above." The words, found in our local newspaper, were those of a grieving father. They were heartfelt, sincere, and a comfort to many who were present.

But they fell far short of the true hope in which we live as followers of Christ.

And they were simply, and sadly, wrong.

Now, I want to be careful here and sensitive to the feelings and convictions of those who have lost loved ones. But I also want to speak clearly and precisely, because Scripture both counters our misunderstandings as well as brings us new and true understandings, and thus hope and encouragement, which far exceed those so often offered up by our popular culture.

---

[1] The Apostles' Creed also affirms the resurrection of the dead in its third article, though it uses the phrase "resurrection of the body": "I believe in the Holy Spirit, the holy Christian church, the communion of saints, the forgiveness of sins, the resurrection of the body, and the life everlasting." The reference here is not to Jesus' Resurrection; that was covered earlier in the second article of the Creed ("On the third day, he rose again"). Rather, here in the third article, the focus is on the life and the hope of the believer.

What the Bible Doesn't Say

Let's begin simply by noting that the Bible nowhere suggests that people ever become angels.[2] Angels are angels and people are people, and, quite frankly, we wouldn't want to be angels. They are simply messengers. Indeed, in the Old Testament there is no special word for "angel" (as there is in the New); rather, there is just the word *mal'ak* which is sometimes translated "messenger" and other times "angel."[3]

Indeed, according to 1 Peter 1:12, that which is reserved for us (and not for the angels) is so great that the angels would like even to get a *glimpse* of it:

> It was revealed to them [the Old Testament prophets] that they were not serving themselves, but you, in these things which now have been announced to you through those who preached the gospel to you by the Holy Spirit sent from heaven—things into which angels long to look.

The Bible also doesn't say that we have immortal souls. That's

---

[2]In Mark 12:25 (and the parallels in Matthew 22:30 and Luke 20:36), Jesus at one point says that those who rise from the dead "are like angels in heaven," but the important word here is "like." "For when they rise from the dead, they neither marry nor are given in marriage, but are like angels in heaven." Jesus is here arguing against the Sadducees who deny the resurrection of the body. His point is that, just as angels do not marry, so those who are raised from the dead will not marry in heaven. He is not saying that we will become angels. (And neither, as a careful reading of his words shows, is he getting into the question of whether marriages entered into on earth will continue in heaven ... a matter best left in the hands of God.)

[3] In Genesis 32:1-3, the word *mal'ak* appears twice and is usually translated "angels" in verse 1 and "messengers" in verse 3. But this is merely the choice of the translators.

another popular misunderstanding and confusion: the opinion that, when we die, our souls float off heavenward while our bodies are buried in the ground to molder away.[4] Oh, our bodies are indeed buried and do molder (or are perhaps cremated), but, according to Scripture, that's not the end of them.

The idea of "immortal souls" comes to us from the Greek world in which Christianity arose. The Greeks generally emphasized the purity and importance of the spirit, and they at times denigrated that which was "merely" physical, such as the body and its appetites. Plato and others used the phrase *soma sema*, meaning the body (*soma*) is a prison (*sema*) of the soul.

This sense that the soul is freed by death to soar away from the body is one not found in the Bible, but it has a long history of traveling *alongside* orthodox Christian teaching – sort of like the "fall of Satan" story we looked at in chapter 2.

… and What It Does

Now, whereas the Bible doesn't mention the "immortality of the soul," it does speak repeatedly of the resurrection of the dead and of a time when we, having been bodily resurrected, will *become* immortal.[5] *That's* the hope in which we live.

---

[4] With a few rare exceptions, the Old Testament doesn't yet know of or look for life after death. Thus, we will find texts such as Ecclesiastes 12:7 suggesting that, in death, "the dust will return to the earth as it was, and the spirit will return to God who gave it" – the futility of which is immediately decried in the next verse: "Vanity of vanities," says the Preacher, "all is vanity!"

[5] The words "immortal" and "immortality" appear only six times in the

What's the difference? Immortality of the soul suggests our souls sort of float on after our bodies are buried and rot away – an idea that is almost as tiresome as the cartoon image of us as angels with wings and haloes sitting on the edge of a cloud strumming a harp. Neither is particularly dynamic or exciting to contemplate.

Resurrection of the dead, on the other hand, means that when we die we are really dead and then, at the end of the age, God will raise us up. Body and soul will again be united. As God intended us to be at the beginning, so we shall be at the end – which, when you think about it, should not be all that surprising. God's basic will for us does not change. I'll say more about this in a later chapter.

The promise of the resurrection of the dead – of *our* bodily resurrection – is mentioned again and again in the New Testament. It is different from Jesus' Resurrection, but it is *based and grounded* upon his Resurrection. Because Jesus was raised from the dead, so, we too, have that same hope.[6] Paul argues this point strongly in **1 Corinthians 15**, confronting those who were saying, "Yes, Jesus was raised from the dead ... but we won't be." Beginning in verse 12, he writes:

Bible: Romans 2:7; 1 Corinthians 15:53-54; 1 Timothy 1:17; 6:16; and 2 Timothy 1:10. The Bible says that God alone is immortal (1 Timothy 6:16), but speaks of a day when we, as resurrected creatures, will "put on immortality" (1 Corinthians 15:53-54).

[6] Thus, when the first martyr Stephen was dying and cried out, "Lord Jesus, receive my spirit" (Acts 7:59), this no more denied hope for *his* resurrection than Jesus' cry to the Father, "Into your hands I commit my spirit" denied his own approaching Easter Resurrection.

> Now if Christ is preached, that He has been raised from the
> dead, how do some among you say that there is no
> resurrection of the dead? But if there is no resurrection of
> the dead, not even Christ has been raised; and if Christ has
> not been raised, then our preaching is vain, your faith also is
> vain. ... if Christ has not been raised, your faith is worthless;
> you are still in your sins.

The discussion was not a new one. A split had developed in Judaism between the Pharisees, who believed in the resurrection of the dead, and the Sadducees, who did not. Jesus agreed with the Pharisees on this point.

In **Mark 12:18-27**[7], the Sadducees try to trap Jesus with a contrived story of a woman who marries one of seven brothers and then, when he dies, marries each brother, one after another, as they, in turn also die. (One wonders why, when brothers two, three and four die after marrying this woman, brothers five, six and seven didn't sense something was amiss; but I digress.) Jesus tells the Sadducees that they are "greatly mistaken," noting that God is God of the living and not the dead, and that God's own claim to be God of Abraham, Isaac and Jacob shows that they must then, in some way, still be alive.

In **John 11:23-27**, Lazarus dies. Jesus tells his sister, Martha, "Your brother will rise again." Not understanding that Jesus meant this was about to happen right then, Martha replies, "I know that he will rise again in the resurrection on the last day." There it is again! – that hope of resurrection of the dead. Jesus himself hadn't yet been raised from the dead, so Martha wasn't thinking of that. Rather, she was already living in that hope of bodily resurrection in

---

[7] See also the parallel references in Matt. 22:23-33 and Luke 20:27–40.

which we also live today. Jesus affirms her belief in that last day event, which is promised for all of us, but then he went on to do what he had come to do that day: resuscitate her brother Lazarus as a "foretaste" of what was to come.[8]

This hope continues throughout the rest of the New Testament. It was not merely the preaching of "life after death" that got the disciples in trouble after the day of Pentecost. In **Acts 4:1-2**, we read:

> As they were speaking to the people, the priests and the captain of the temple guard and the Sadducees came up to them, being greatly disturbed because they were teaching the people and proclaiming in Jesus the resurrection from the dead.

For the secular Greeks of Athens, the issue was not theological but rather philosophical. At the end of Paul's Areopagus sermon, we read of their mixed response in **Acts 17:32**:

> Now when they heard of the resurrection of the dead, some began to sneer, but others said, "We shall hear you again concerning this."

It is clear also, in Paul's letters, that the resurrection of the dead – not merely souls flitting off to heaven – is central to his message. His earliest statements are found in **1 Thessalonians** (which we will consider in more detail in the next chapter). There, in **chapter 4, verse 16**, he notes that, when Christ returns at the

---

[8] It is important to note that the raising of Lazarus was a resuscitation, not "resurrection of the body." Lazarus eventually died again, but resurrection of the body, at the end of the age, is a "once forever" event. Thus, I describe the raising of Lazarus as a "foretaste" of that event.

end of the age, "the dead in Christ will rise first."

In **Romans 8:11**, he proclaims that "He who raised Christ Jesus from the dead will also give life to your mortal bodies." We have already considered his strong defense of resurrection of the dead in 1 Corinthians 15. Earlier in that letter, in **1 Corinthians 6:14**, he affirms that "God has not only raised the Lord, but will also raise us up through His power," an affirmation found again in **2 Corinthians 4:14 and 5:1-9.**[9]

In **Philippians 3:10-11**, Paul's greatest desire is

> that I may know [Christ] and the power of His resurrection and the fellowship of His sufferings, being conformed to His death; in order that I may attain to the resurrection from the dead.

And ten verses later, he tells how "the Lord Jesus Christ … will transform the body of our humble state into conformity with the body of His glory." This clarifies his earlier (1:23) contrast between his "desire to depart and be with Christ" and his

---

[9] This latter reference is somewhat complex. It describes our resurrection bodies not merely in terms of a reconstitution of our present bodies, described merely as "tents," but rather as being "houses" which are at present awaiting us "in the heavens." Interestingly, the text does not say that we will go there to receive them, but rather that they will be sent here to "clothe" us – even that our present bodies will be "swallowed up" by these future bodies which are described as "life."

Exactly how we are to understand this is not clear but, until that time, "while we are at home in the body we are absent from the Lord" – perhaps in the sense that we at present can only "see in a mirror dimly, but then face to face" (1 Corinthians 13:12). I will say more about the possible location of our future home in the chapter on "Where Is Heaven?"

realization that to "remain in the body" was needful for them. Rather than suggesting that his ultimate destination was to be some state apart from his (resurrected) body, his point was merely to recognize that, for the moment, it was important for him to remain in this present world for their sake – and that ultimately he will "attain to the resurrection from the dead."

Finally, when Paul is arrested and put on trial, it is clear that it is his preaching of the resurrection of the dead which lies at the heart of the accusations made against him. In **Acts 23:6**, finding himself before a group comprised of both Pharisees and Sadducees, Paul cries out, "I am on trial for the hope and resurrection of the dead!" And when he was then brought before the Roman governor, Felix, he boldly affirms that "there shall certainly be a resurrection of both the righteous and the wicked" (**Acts 24:25**) and repeats his earlier claim that "For the resurrection of the dead I am on trial before you today" (**Acts 24:21**).

When All Is Said and Done

All of these texts should make it clear that belief in the resurrection of the dead or resurrection of the body (as distinctly opposed to immortality of the soul or our becoming angels) is more than just an incidental matter. N. T. Wright has put it well:

> If we squeeze [bodily resurrection] to the margins, as many have done by implication, or indeed, if we leave it out altogether, as some have done quite explicitly, we don't just lose an extra feature, like buying a car that happens not to have electrically operated mirrors. We lose the central

engine, which drives it and gives every other component its reason for working.[10]

What is so interesting is that this hope of resurrection of the body was there from the Church's very beginnings – all the way up through the 18th century. Again it is N. T. Wright who observes this – though in a different reference than the one which I just quoted. He notes that, prior to the end of the 18th century, tombstone engravings generally bore statements such as "I lie here awaiting the day of resurrection." Near the end of the 18th century, however, and continuing to today, there is a move to expressions such as "I am no longer here; my soul has gone to heaven."[11]

---

[10] N. T. Wright, "Heaven Is Not Our Home," *Christianity Today*, March 24, 2008 at http://www.christianitytoday.com/ct/2008/april/13.36.html. The subject of his provocative title will be considered in chapter 7 of this book.

[11] Wright notes:

> The Western Church has been fixated on going to heaven and has lost its grip on the resurrection and on the embodiedness of the future life. When I worked at Westminster Abbey I noticed that tombstones before about 1780 or so would often say things about the resurrection: "I'm resting here at the moment but I'll be back, I shall arise." Through the 19th century and on into the 20th century you don't get that. Instead you get: "Gone home to be with Jesus" or "Heaven is my home." It's important to give comfort to people so they know that the loved one who died is with Jesus, but the whole of the New Testament insists that's not the end of the story. There will be a new day, a new world, a new creation and new bodies to live in it. When you say this, people sort of scratch their heads and say, "Yeah, I guess I sort of believe that but I really thought it was just about going to heaven." It's really time to get a grip because it affects everything else: how we do ethics, how we do politics, it plays out in a whole range of things.

Why is this matter so important? It's important because it's "joined at the hip," as it were, with the matter of where God intends our "life after death" to take place. Is it to be in heaven? Or might the Bible just point in another direction? Might the divine precincts of heaven be a bad match for bodily resurrected folks? And, if such be the case, what might be a better – and more biblical – destination?

That will be the subject of the seventh chapter of this book. But before we get there, we need to look at the interim issue of Christ's return at the end of the age and what happens if you get "left behind."

Found in Dick Tripp, *The Biblical Mandate for Caring for Creation* (Eugene, Oregon: Wipf & Stock, 2013) 129. Tripp attributes the quotation to "an interview in *Christianity Today* but does not give the issue, page or date.

And What Do You Say? Questions for Discussion

1. The chapter begins with some popular (but non-biblical) views of what happens to us when we die. What are they?

2. What is the difference between "immortality of the soul" and "resurrection of the body." Which one is found in the Bible and confessed by the Church? (Review what was said in the chapter's first footnote regarding the Apostles' Creed.)

3. A change took place, near the end of the 18th century, regarding the popular view of life after death. What was the change and why is it significant?

4. In anticipation of the book's seventh chapter, the present chapter concludes with several questions including, "Might the divine precincts of heaven be a bad match for bodily resurrected folks?" What is the issue being raised here? What do you think at this point?

5. Can you step back from all the varied discussions of what heaven (or the "new earth") will be like for us and grasp the magnitude of God's overall promise for us in Scripture? What is a simple and clear statement of that promise?

6. What If You Get "Left Behind"?
"As It Was in the Days of Noah ...."

> Then there will be two men in the field; one will be taken and one will be left. Two women will be grinding at the mill; one will be taken and one will be left. Therefore be on the alert, for you do not know which day your Lord is coming.
>
> Matthew 24:40-42

> Then we who are alive and remain will be caught up together with them in the clouds to meet the Lord in the air, and so we shall always be with the Lord.
>
> 1 Thessalonians 4:17

This could easily become the longest chapter in the book – or an entire book of its own – but it won't. I want simply to look at one particular element in the midst of a very complex, and at times convoluted, discussion.

Beginning in 1995, Tim LaHaye and Jerry B. Jenkins published a sequence of 16 best-selling novels known as the "Left Behind" series. The books led to a series of films and even video games, and most of this will be well-known to those familiar with terms such as eschatology, the Rapture, Dispensationalism, the Tribulation, Premillennialism, and so on. The books and films (and, I suppose, even the video games) have been both affirmed as well as derided among both Christians as well as non-Christians, so you may well have an opinion on the subject![1]

---

[1] There is even a "Left Behind" website: www.leftbehind.com, on which you will find all the books and movies.

I do not want to open this can of worms completely. When it comes to matters such as Millennialism and pre-Tribulation Rapture vs mid-Trib and post-Trib, I find myself in sympathy with an opinion I once encountered many years ago as a student. A speaker had just tried to introduce us to an overview of all of these eschatological positions and our eyes were beginning to glaze over. Finally, someone had the temerity to ask, "And just what is *your* opinion on all of this?" … to which the speaker replied, "Me? I'm a Pan-Millennialist." Our hearts sank at the introduction of one more term. "So," the overwhelmed questioner asked, "what's a Pan-Millennialist?" "I believe," the speaker replied, "that God is going to make it all pan out in the end."

Amen and amen. It's not that I don't think these matters are important; it's just that I don't think that our getting them all sorted out precisely is salvation-critical. That is to say, on this particular issue we can differ and even afford to be wrong. They are not anywhere near as critical as are die-for issues such as the Divinity of Christ or the Resurrection, and they are certainly not matters over which we should excommunicate one another!

However, one piece of this body of end-of-the-world scenarios *has*, in recent years, caused stress in some people's lives. This is the matter of the Rapture, an event which is the basis for the entire "Left Behind" series of books and movies. The Rapture is the snatching away to heaven of God's faithful people just before, during or after various end-time events. In the books and movies, the Rapture is portrayed very dramatically with Christians suddenly disappearing and those who are "left behind" having to deal with driverless cars and crashing planes.

What the Bible Doesn't Say

It's sometimes pointed out that the word "rapture" does not occur in the Bible; but, then, one may point out in response, neither does the word "Trinity" and yet the Trinity *is* a core element of Christian faith.

In the case of the word "rapture," it's like the word "hell" in the Apostle's Creed which we discussed in chapter four: it comes from a word used in the Latin translation of the Bible known as the Vulgate. In this case, it is found in 1 Thessalonians 4:17, quoted at the beginning of this chapter. There, we read that, when Christ comes again, we will be "caught up" in the clouds. The Latin for "caught up" is *rapiemur*, from the verb *rapio* which is related to the noun *raptura*.

So there you have the etymology of the word; thus, yes, it's fair to talk about "the rapture" in the Bible.

The question, however, is what Paul had in mind when he used this verb to describe this end-times event. We need, therefore, to start with what Jesus said earlier.[2]

---

[2] Those who have studied the historical background of the New Testament will be aware that the *writing* of the letters of Paul took place earlier than the *writing* of the Gospels (and that 1 Thessalonians is probably the first of Paul's letters). However, the *events* portrayed in the (later) Gospels took place prior to Paul's ministry and the writing of his letters, and these events – Jesus' ministry and teaching – form the foundation and starting point for what Paul has to say. Thus, we look at Jesus statements first.

... and What It Does

Jesus' words in **Matthew 24-25**, along with **Mark 13** and **Luke 21**, are sometimes called the "Little Apocalypse" because they give the most detailed account of his end-time teaching. In addition, **Luke 17** also contains these themes. These verses do not mention "rapture" (that is, words such as *rapiemur, rapio,* or *raptura*), but it is here that we find mention of being "taken" and "left."

Mark 13:26-27 is the oldest[3] of these texts and notes a "gathering" (though without mentioning those who are "left behind"):

> And then they will see the Son of man coming in clouds with great power and glory. And then he will send out the angels, and gather his elect from the four winds, from the ends of the earth to the ends of heaven.

Jesus is here describing his return in the language of Daniel 7:13-14,[4] and this language, along with mention of a "gathering," is also found in **Matthew 24:31**.

---

[3] Mark is considered, by most students of the New Testament, to be the first of the Gospels to be written. Matthew and Luke later used portions of what Mark wrote, plus other material, in compiling their accounts. John writes from a rather different perspective and does not share material in the same way that the other three do.

[4] "I kept looking in the night visions, and behold, with the clouds of heaven One like a Son of Man was coming, and He came up to the Ancient of Days and was presented before Him. And to Him was given dominion, Glory and a kingdom, that all the peoples, nations and men of every language might serve Him. His dominion is an everlasting dominion which will not pass away; and His kingdom is one which will not be destroyed."

Luke 21:27-28 also refers to the Daniel text, though makes no mention of a "gathering" or of people being "taken" or "left." In verse 8, however, it does give a piece of good advice regarding end time discussions: "See to it that you are not misled"!

It is in Luke 17 and Matthew 24 that we find mentions of people being "taken" and "left." In **Luke 17:34-36**, Jesus, speaking of the day (and night) of his return, says:

> I tell you, on that night there will be two in one bed; one will be taken and the other will be left. There will be two women grinding at the same place; one will be taken and the other will be left. Two men will be in the field; one will be taken and the other will be left.

In **Matthew 24.40-42**, the message is similar:

> Then there will be two men in the field; one will be taken and one will be left. Two women will be grinding at the mill; one will be taken and one will be left. Therefore be on the alert, for you do not know which day your Lord is coming.

If one comes to these verses with "rapture" in mind, one will assume that the goal is to be "taken" so as not to be found among those who are "left." But here, both the language[5] and the context are critically important. If we read the preceding verses, beginning in verse 36, it soon becomes apparent that being "taken" is the fate of the faithless. (Below, I have boldfaced the critical phrases.) Again, keep in mind that Jesus is speaking of when the end will

---

[5] Here, the words "will be taken" are not found in the Latin text of the Vulgate as *rapiemur* or *rapio*, from which the word "rapture" comes. Rather, the Vulgate uses *adsumetur*. That being said, the text still speaks of people being "taken." Thus, the issue is whether it is better to be taken or left, and it is the context which decides that.

come:

> But of that day and hour no one knows, not even the angels of heaven, nor the Son, but the Father alone. For the coming of the Son of Man will be just like the days of Noah. For as in those days before the flood they were eating and drinking, marrying and giving in marriage, until the day that Noah entered the ark, and they did not understand **until the flood came and took them all away**; so will the coming of the Son of Man be. Then there will be two men in the field; **one will be taken and one will be left**. "Two women will be grinding at the mill; **one will be taken and one will be left**. "Therefore be on the alert, for you do not know which day your Lord is coming.

"... until the flood came and took them all away." Jesus uses the time of Noah as his example – a time in which people were "taken away" to destruction while Noah and his family were "left behind," as it were. Jesus then goes immediately to speak of those who will be taken or left at the end of the age. As it was in the days of Noah (in which being "taken" meant being destroyed), "so will the coming of the Son of Man be. ... one will be taken and one will be left." It appears, from what Jesus says, that when the end comes we would *want* to be among those "left behind"!

And there is more. We now come to the only text which actually mentions "rapture" – **1 Thessalonians 4:13-18**, which I touched upon at the beginning of our discussion:

> [13]But we do not want you to be uninformed, brethren, about those who are asleep, so that you will not grieve as do the rest who have no hope. [14]For if we believe that Jesus died and rose again, even so God will bring with Him those who have fallen asleep in Jesus. [15]For this we say to you by the word of the Lord, that we who are alive and remain until the coming of the Lord, will not precede those who have fallen

asleep. [16]For the Lord Himself will descend from heaven with a shout, with the voice of the archangel and with the trumpet of God, and the dead in Christ will rise first. [17]Then we who are alive and remain will be caught up (*rapiemur*) together with them in the clouds to meet the Lord in the air, and so we shall always be with the Lord. [18]Therefore comfort one another with these words.

What is interesting about this text is that it doesn't say what will happen – or where we will go – *after* we are "caught up" in the clouds … other than the fact that we shall, from that point on, "always be with the Lord."

The clue may be found in the "voice of the archangel" and the "trumpet of God." What we may actually have here is a vertical representation of something which the people of Paul's day often saw on a horizontal plane: a royal or state visit by an important personage. When someone of great importance – a king, let us say – paid a visit to a town or village, it was a major event. It involved a procession as the king approached, and people were expected to stop what they were doing and take note. To help make that happen, the procession was preceded by a trumpeter and a herald who would be shouting, "Here comes the king!" The people would pour out from the town and line the roads. Then, as the king and his retinue drew near, they would join the procession and the whole group, now rather sizeable, would enter the town together.

It appears this is what Paul has in mind when he writes. He uses this image because he knew his readers would understand it. We, on the other hand, living in an age when presidents arrive in large jets, have to have Paul's imagery explained to us.

Assuming this is, indeed, what Paul is doing – describing the

return of Christ using the imagery of a king paying a royal visit –
then, once, again, we may want to rethink *our* image of "rapture."

Again, note that Paul doesn't say what happens *after* Christ
descends from heaven and we are "caught up" to "meet the Lord in
the air," except that "we shall always be with the Lord." If he is,
indeed, using the image of a royal visit, however, his readers would
expect that the next step would be for all of us, having "met the
Lord in the air," not to remain there with him – and certainly not to
accompany him back to the place from which he had come – but
rather then to accompany him as he continues his earthward
descent to enter our "town" – known as planet Earth!

But if *that* be the case, then what about heaven? When do we
go there? Or ... *will* we go there?

That's the subject of our next chapter.

And What Do You Say? Questions for Discussion

1. Have you read any of the "Left Behind" books or seen any movies based upon them? What is their general premise?

2. How important do you think it is for us to have a clear understanding of how the end times are going to unfold? What do you think of the response of the speaker who described himself as a "Pan-Millennialist"?

3. What have you heard and thought about the stories in which "one will be taken and the other will be left" as found in Matthew 24 and Luke 17? How does this chapter suggest that context – the reading of passages before and after the passage of interest – should affect our understanding of these "left behind" texts?

4. The background of the times is also important in understanding texts. 1 Thessalonians 4 describes Christ descending from heaven and being met by his faithful people in the air. Paul doesn't say where they will then go and he apparently assumes that the reader will know. What is the answer often assumed today? What alternative is suggested in the chapter, based on a practice of Paul's day?

5. Again, as asked in the questions at the end of the previous chapter, can you step back from the complexities and varying opinions regarding "left behind" and grasp the magnitude of God's overall intentions for us in Scripture? What is a simple and clear statement of those intentions?

7. Where Is Heaven? ... and When?
Some Informed Speculation

> Then I saw a new heaven and a new earth; for the first
> heaven and the first earth passed away, and there is no
> longer *any* sea. And I saw the holy city, new Jerusalem,
> coming down out of heaven from God, made ready as a bride
> adorned for her husband. And I heard a loud voice from the
> throne, saying, "Behold, the tabernacle of God is among
> men, and He will dwell among them, and they shall be His
> people, and God Himself will be among them, and He will
> wipe away every tear from their eyes; and there will no
> longer be *any* death; there will no longer be *any* mourning,
> or crying, or pain; the first things have passed away."
>
> Revelation 21:1-4

"So where is Auntie Joan right now?" The question was asked by Willie, a puzzled and anxious four-year-old, as the funeral service reached its conclusion. "She's in heaven with Jesus, Willie." And that was the right answer at the right time. Little Willie needed to know, of a certainty, that when we die – and when those we love die – we are in the good and gracious hands of God, and that's a good and safe and wonderful place to be.

But more can be said. What will not change, in the paragraphs that lie ahead, is my absolute conviction that when we die we, indeed, will find ourselves immediately in the good and gracious hands of God and that that's a good and safe and wonderful place to be.

But *where* will that be? And when? In the Bible we find Jesus telling the thief on the cross, "Today, you will be with me in paradise." That sounds fairly immediate. But, as we saw in chapter 5, the Bible also repeatedly speaks of the resurrection of the dead on the last day. Can both be true?

The simple answer, I think, is yes. But I add the "I think" because, toward the end of this chapter, I am going to do a bit of speculating. That's not because the Bible doesn't speak to the matter. It does. Rather, I add the "I think" because, upon closer inspection, I find the Bible moving in a direction you and I may not expect. And it's all to the good.

What the Bible Doesn't Say

As far as I can see, the Bible never comes out and says that we are going to heaven. (I thought of subtitling this chapter "I'm Pretty Sure I'm Not Going to Heaven" but felt that might be disturbing to some – or might perhaps wrongly confirm the opinions of some others!) Rather, our prospects, as found in the Bible, are actually much more promising than that. (And so another "runner up" subtitle for the chapter was "Better Than Heaven!")

Here's the short version. On the one hand, the Bible doesn't speak of our going to heaven. We have been created physical, earthbound creatures, and will one day be raised again as such; yet heaven is – and always has been and always will be – a spiritual realm, God's "control room" as others have put it. Thus, we would be fish out of water in heaven. On the other hand, the Bible *does* speak of a "new earth" that gets far too little attention from most of us.

Now, I certainly can't ask you just to take my word for this.

So let's take a look at what the Bible does say about heaven.

... and What It Does

IN GENERAL

The word "Heaven" is found some 450 times in the Bible, half of those in the New Testament. In some of those references, the word "heaven" is just a euphemism for the word "God." Why a euphemism? Because many pious Jews felt that it was wrong ever to speak the name of God, and so they would say something else. In the Old Testament, for instance, there is a clear movement away from speaking or even writing the divine name Yahweh. Thus, it is often replaced in the Hebrew text with a word that means "Lord."[1] To some extent, this continues in the New Testament where the phrase "kingdom of heaven" is simply as another way of saying "kingdom of God."

If we read carefully, we discover that heaven is God's realm, and people are not found there. For instance, at one point, in the book of Revelation, John is invited up to heaven to see "what must take place after these things" (**Revelation 4:1**). However, in the very next verse he says, "Immediately I was in the Spirit" (or "in the spirit"[2]), indicating that his presence in heaven was spiritual or

---

[1] Even today, when I exchange emails with Orthodox Jews, I find that they write "G-d" and "L-rd," imitating another characteristic move found in Biblical Hebrew: the dropping of the vowels from the name "Yahweh."

[2] The original Greek of the New Testament was written in all upper case (capital) letters. (Likewise, the Hebrew of the Old Testament has only one form of letter; that is, Hebrew has neither upper nor lower case.) Thus, whether or not a word is capitalized in the Bible is purely the decision of the translators.

visionary but not physical. And he didn't stay there ... or else he never could have written the book of Revelation for us.

Yet the popular understanding is that heaven is our destiny. Surely, this must be because there are many verses which support that impression – or at least appear to do so. And indeed there are.

IN THE GOSPELS

In the Gospels, one can point to verses such as Matthew 5:12, 6:19-20 and 19:21 (and their parallels[3]) in which we are told that our "reward" or "treasure" is in heaven. There is also Jesus' promise to the thief on the cross in Luke 23:42-43, which I have already mentioned. There, he says, "Today, you shall be with me in Paradise" – clearly a reference to the afterlife. Let's look a little more closely at each of these texts.

As always, of course, it's important to read such verses carefully. The danger for all students of the Bible is that we tend to bring our expectations to the text and then "find" them there in our reading,[4] rather than listening so intently to the text that *it* reshapes *our* expectations. For instance, in the first of the texts I list above, **Matthew 5:12; 6:19-20 and 19:21**, note that, although our

---

[3] In many places, the Gospels – especially Matthew, Mark and Luke – share language and stories between them. These are known as "parallels," and in this case I am referring to verses such as Mark 10:21, Luke 6:23, 12:33 and 18.22 which also contain Jesus' mentions of reward or treasure in heaven.

[4] Young seminarians are warned, early on, of the dangers of "eisegesis" – that is, of reading one's own opinion *into* the text – as opposed to proper "exegesis," which is reading *out* of the text that which it means to say. Even the best of us can fall prey to eisegesis in spite of our best intentions.

"treasure" or "reward" are in heaven, it does not say that *we* will be there. The point seems to be that heaven is the present repository of that which we are later destined to receive – just as a bank may, at present, be holding an inheritance which will eventually come to you, although you will never go to live in the bank. (We find the same image in **1 Peter 1:4** which speaks of our one day receiving an "inheritance ... reserved in heaven for you.")

Luke 16:19-31 brings us Jesus' parable of the rich man and Lazarus, and many suppose that this parable gives us a graphic image of the afterlife. Jesus' point, however, is not the geography of heaven and hell (neither of which are mentioned, by the way[5]). Rather, his point is that if people refuse to listen to God's word then they won't be impressed even if someone comes back from the dead. We can't really push the parable beyond that.

Jesus' promise of Paradise in **Luke 23:42-43** is rather different and is most interesting on two counts. First, this promise is spoken specifically to the thief on the cross, so we may want to be cautious about applying it in general to all of us. But second, and more to the point, Jesus uses a word – *paradeisos* in the Greek text – which is different from the word used for heaven (*ouranos*). It is found in only two other places in the New Testament: 2 Corinthians 12:4 (where Paul speaks of being "caught up into *paradeisos*," apparently in a vision – a reference which could refer to heaven) and Revelation 2:7 (in which *paradeisos* is associated with the tree of life – the tree found in the garden of Eden and

---

[5] Jesus mentions just "Abraham's bosom/side" and "Hades," the latter, as we noted earlier, being the same as "Sheol," the place of the dead, not Hell.

discussed in chapter 3). I will discuss both of these texts below.

With only these three references to *paradeisos* in the New Testament, and none of them really explained, the word is left untranslated in English Bibles and is simply transliterated[6] as "Paradise." Yet Jesus, and perhaps the thief on the cross, knew what the word meant because of its occurrences in the Old Testament. It was originally a Persian word, and it makes three rare appearances in the Hebrew text as *pardes*[7]. In the context of these three occurrences, *pardes* means something like a "special garden of the king."

But there is more. I've only mentioned the (original) Hebrew text of the Old Testament. At the time of Jesus, Greek had come to be the dominant language around the Mediterranean, and the Old Testament had been translated into this language about 250 years earlier. This translation, known as the Septuagint, was very popular, and in it the word *paradeisos* was used for the Garden of Eden not only in Genesis 2 and 3 but also in Isaiah, Ezekiel and Joel.[8] If this is what Jesus had in mind, it is most interesting because it appears that, at this moment, when he points to the afterlife, he points not up but back – back to that original setting in

---

[6] To transliterate a word is simply to take its sound in one language and reproduce that sound (rather than its meaning) in another. We saw that earlier with the word *gehenna* in the Vulgate. The most famous transliteration in the Bible is the Hebrew word *halleluyah* which is actually the imperative of the Hebrew verb *halal*, with a direct object (*yah* for *Yahweh*) added at the end. Another is Messiah, which is just an English language pronunciation of the Hebrew word *meshiach*, which means "anointed one."

[7] Nehemiah 2:8; Ecclesiastes 2:5 and Song of Solomon 4:13.

[8] Isaiah 51:3; Ezekiel 28:13; 31:8; 31:9; Joel 2:3.

the Garden of Eden before the fall. I'll say more about this later.

In **John 14:2-3**, Jesus tells his disciples, "In My Father's house are many dwelling places; ... I go to prepare a place for you." Again, we must note that there is no mention of heaven. In Genesis, the place God has designed for us is described as a garden, and, as we shall see below, in Revelation as a city come down *from* heaven. Here in John Jesus describes it as a "house." What is common to all three of these images is their familiar earthbound language, language which reveals a consistency in the way scripture speaks of God's intended future for his people.

IN THE LETTERS OF PAUL

Paul mentions heaven 18 times,[9] and often speaks of it either as the realm or abode of God[10] or as the place *from* which Christ has come or will come.[11]

Of these references, the most interesting is the one in which Paul speaks of actually going to heaven: **2 Corinthians 12:2-4**, which I mentioned above because of his reference to Paradise (*paradeisos*):

> I know a man in Christ who fourteen years ago—whether in the body I do not know, or out of the body I do not know, God knows—such a man was caught up to the third heaven.

---

[9] Two references are in Ephesians and four in Colossians. I know that some question whether Paul wrote these letters but that debate has no bearing on our discussion. Even if Paul did not write them, they are still Scripture and thus part of God's revelation to us.

[10] Romans 1:8; 1 Corinthians 8:5; Ephesians 6:9; Colossians 4:1.

[11] Romans 10:6-7; 1 Corinthians 15:47; 1 Thessalonians 1:10; 4:16; 2 Thessalonians 1:7.

> And I know how such a man—whether in the body or apart from the body I do not know, God knows— was caught up into Paradise and heard inexpressible words, which a man is not permitted to speak.

There is much we don't know here. Most students of the Bible agree that when Paul says "I know a man in Christ" he is likely referring to himself and describing an experience of his own. Was it "in the body" or was it visionary? I suspect it was the latter, but Paul appears not to be sure himself and so we have to leave the matter open. We also don't know what he means by "the third heaven," though he appears to connect it with Paradise. We can't simply dismiss this passage as "odd"—it is Scripture, after all. But it is rather an outlier in terms of Paul's other mentions of heaven.

In other places, Paul, like Jesus, will speak of heaven not as the place *to* which we will go but rather as the repository *from* which we will receive our inheritance in the age to come. For instance, in **2 Corinthians 5:1-4** we are first told that "we have a building from God, a house not made with hands, eternal in the heavens." The next verse, however, speaks of this "building" one day coming to us *from* heaven rather than our going there to possess it. That is, we are described, in verse 2, as "longing to be clothed with our dwelling from (Greek *ex*, literally "out of") heaven" – a most unusual imagery, yet one which fits very well with everything we have seen so far in terms of heaven as the repository or source of what we will one day receive.

Philippians 3:20[12] does the same, first noting that "our

------

[12] A few verses before this text, in Philippians 3:14, Paul speaks of awaiting God's "upward (Greek ἄνω) call." This could

citizenship is in heaven" but then immediately adding "*from* which also we eagerly wait for a Savior, the Lord Jesus Christ." And just as Jesus spoke of a "treasure" or "reward" being laid up for us in heaven, so **Colossians 1:5** refers to "the hope laid up for you in heaven."

Now, so far, from what I read in scripture, I am suggesting that heaven is the realm of God; that it is a spiritual realm in which resurrected creatures, such as we will be, would not fit particularly well. At the same time, heaven is described as the present "repository" of our future "treasure" or "reward."

SOMETHING NEW AND SUPRISING

Now, where does all this go? I think it goes somewhere which, for most of us, is very new and surprising – and encouraging. At the same time, it goes somewhere very old – as old as Isaiah the prophet. Isaiah is a rather complex book, and Christians often – and for good reason – look with interest to its messianic prophecies. But Isaiah brings us much more in addition to that, and, in the last two chapters of the book, we come to a promise of "a new heavens and a new earth." In **Isaiah 65:17-18**, God says:

---

be understood as a reference to heaven were it not for so many other texts pointing elsewhere, as we are seeing. I would therefore understand this verse pointing not so much to "heaven" as to the Bible's typical view of a "three story universe" in which God is above us and the dead are below (see the earlier discussion of Jesus' "descent into hell"). It is thus unfortunate that the popular NIV and NRSV translate ἄνω as "heavenward." The Greek word simply means "upward" as found in earlier translations such as RSV and NASV.

"For behold, I create new heavens and a new earth; and the former things will not be remembered or come to mind. But be glad and rejoice forever in what I create; for behold, I create Jerusalem *for* rejoicing and her people *for* gladness.

And in **Isaiah 66:22**, God promises that:

"the new heavens and the new earth which I make will endure before Me," declares the LORD.

Now, I imagine you are familiar with the phrase "new earth," but have you given it much thought? For instance, *why a new earth if we are all going to heaven?*

God's promise through Isaiah was not forgotten by followers of Jesus, and in **2 Peter 3:10-13** we read:

But the day of the Lord will come like a thief, in which the heavens will pass away with a roar and the elements will be destroyed with intense heat, and the earth and its works will be burned up. Since all these things are to be destroyed in this way, what sort of people ought you to be in holy conduct and godliness, looking for and hastening the coming of the day of God, because of which the heavens will be destroyed by burning, and the elements will melt with intense heat! But according to His promise we are looking for new heavens and a new earth, in which righteousness dwells.

In passages such as this (for instance, in the book of Revelation), we often focus on the destruction. But, again ... that "new earth." What is to be its purpose?

There are two more passages to examine before I pull all of this together. The first is **Romans 8:18-23**, a passage from Paul which we have not considered so far because it doesn't mention heaven. Yet it is that very lack of mention that makes this passage so interesting:

> ¹⁸For I consider that the sufferings of this present time are not worthy to be compared with the glory that is to be revealed to us. ¹⁹For the anxious longing of the creation waits eagerly for the revealing of the sons of God. ²⁰For the creation was subjected to futility, not willingly, but because of Him who subjected it, in hope ²¹that the creation itself also will be set free from its slavery to corruption into the freedom of the glory of the children of God. ²²For we know that the whole creation groans and suffers the pains of childbirth together until now. ²³And not only this, but also we ourselves, having the first fruits of the Spirit, even we ourselves groan within ourselves, waiting eagerly for *our* adoption as sons, the redemption of our body.

Here, Paul speaks not of heaven but of the "anxious longing of the creation" which will itself "be set free from its slavery to corruption." The creation is not ultimately to be destroyed but rather to be "set free." And Paul then relates this to "the redemption of our body."

The other passage is one which, for me, ties up all of this in a neat package. It comes, not surprisingly, at the very end of the Bible. In the final chapters of the book of Revelation, when all has taken place, and the cycles of bowls and trumpets and seals are completed, and the beast and the false prophet and Death and Hades have all been thrown into the lake of fire, we read a passage which answers the question of *Why a new earth?* In **Revelation 21:1-4**, we read:

> ¹Then I saw a new heaven and a new earth; for the first heaven and the first earth passed away, and there is no longer *any* sea. ²And I saw the holy city, new Jerusalem, coming down out of heaven from God, made ready as a bride

> adorned for her husband. [3]And I heard a loud voice from the throne, saying, "Behold, the tabernacle of God is among men, and He will dwell among them, and they shall be His people, and God Himself will be among them, [4]and He will wipe away every tear from their eyes; and there will no longer be *any* death; there will no longer be *any* mourning, or crying, or pain; the first things have passed away."

There it is, spelled out as clearly as possible. Our eternal destination is described as a "holy city, new Jerusalem, coming down out of heaven from God," at which point we don't go to God in his heaven but rather his "tabernacle" ("dwelling" in other translations) will be among *us*.

GOD'S INTENT DOES NOT CHANGE

So, when all is said and done, the Bible does seem to be saying that our future is not in heaven but rather upon a new earth.[13] And again, when you stop to think about it, is it so strange that God's ultimate intent for us is, for all practical purposes, the same as was his original intent? *God* doesn't change. His original plan for us was described at the beginning of Genesis as earthbound and in a garden. At the end, in the last chapters of the very symbolic book of Revelation, it is described as a city coming down *out* of heaven (think again of Peter's "kept in heaven for you") to a new, or restored, earth. Once again, our residence is described as earthbound, though this time the image is a city instead of a garden.

These two images of Garden and City form, as it were, bookends which enclose the rest of the Bible – bookends which

---

[13] Or a *restored* earth as in Romans 8? I will say more about this possibility in the final chapter.)

sketch out God's intent for us. Each bookend, for instance, includes the tree of life.[14] By the way, the tree of life is found in Revelation not only at the end (chapter 22) but also very near the beginning. In **Revelation 2:7**, the figure of Jesus says:

> To him who overcomes, I will grant to eat of the tree of life which is in the Paradise of God.

Here, the tree of life is connected with Paradise (*paradeisos*) which, as we have seen, is associated with the Garden. Only when we get to the end of Revelation do we find that the tree of life – and thus Paradise – is also to be associated with the City come down out of heaven to the new earth.

A new earth. Those who know me have often heard me say, "*That's* something I can get excited about!" Those cartoonish images I've mentioned (and that's all they are) of people with wings and haloes sitting on the edge of a cloud strumming a harp have absolutely no appeal for me. How tedious that would be!

But think of a new earth, much like this one with all its beauty but without death and disease and potholes and all the rest – without sin! – a world in which we have good and healthy relationships and there are things to do and to explore and to learn. Ah, again, that's something I can get excited about!

In the meantime, heaven remains as the spiritual domain of God – his control room, if you will – the repository in which is stored, and from which will come, all those things described as "treasure" and "hope" which God intends for us.

---

[14] In Genesis, the tree of life is found in 2:9; 3:22,24. It reappears in Revelation at 2:7; 22:1,2,14,19.

A Little Speculation

The question of *when* is still a puzzle. Again, in Luke 23:43 Jesus tells the thief on the cross "today" and yet we also are told to expect the resurrection of the dead at the end of the age (see the many references above in chapter 5). How can it be both ways?

At this point, permit me a little speculation. Speculation is not a bad thing as long as one makes it clear that it *is* speculation. And what I am about to sketch out is at least *suggested* by a number of passages from the Bible. The passages I have in mind include the ones I have just mentioned: Jesus' mention of "today" in Luke 23 and the many references to resurrection of the dead. There is also Jesus' very intriguing statement in John 8:58 that "before Abraham was, I am."

Time. Time is our problem. God is outside of time and we may assume he created it. In any event, when we start dealing with matters such as eternity, or the "end of the age," or a "new heavens and a new earth," we should probably be prepared to be a bit flexible in our understanding of time and of "when."

The image most of us have of time is probably the typical western one:[15] We stand, as it were, facing the future in front of us, with the past lying behind us. Movement through time is thus a forward movement along a line.

------

[15] Having spent quite some time in Africa, I am also intrigued by the traditional African view of time: that we face looking into the past and backing into the future. This makes rather good sense, when you think about it, since we can "see" the past but have no access to the future except as we stumble "backwards" into it.

But where is eternity? Oh, I suppose we might consider the line to be infinite in length and that at some point in the distant future we enter eternity. Eternity is on the same line – just a long way down the road and continuing forever. When we die, God somehow "jumps" us from where we are to that point way down the line to where eternity begins. Perhaps that point is what is known as judgment day.

But what if – and here is my speculation – what if, invisible to us all, there is, as it were, a thin curtain immediately to our left as we move along the line of time? On the other side of the curtain lies eternity – to our left, not ahead of us. And what if death then involves not a jump further down the line but rather a sudden and immediate left turn such that we penetrate the curtain and find ourselves in eternity?

In this case, eternity begins at the curtain and moves forever to the left. At any point along the line of time, one may suddenly die and take a "left turn" through the curtain and enter the new world – the new earth? – of eternity.

What is intriguing to me about this very speculative picture is that it fits both with Jesus' "today" to the thief on the cross as well as with the Bible's statements about resurrection of the dead. We all die at different times, but we all find ourselves entering eternity at the same "time" – "today" – at eternity's "year one" as it were.

And I have this image of my death as suddenly taking a left, passing through that curtain, and then looking around for the first time at what is now going to occupy me forever. And there, off to what is now my new left I see Abraham, also near the curtain. I walk over to him and say, "Abraham, this place is *fantastic*! Tell me about it." And Abraham replies, "I don't really know. I just got here myself." And then, pointing to one with nail-scarred hands, he'll say, "You'll have to talk to *Him*." To the one who said, "Before Abraham was, I am."

I so look forward to that conversation!

And What Do You Say? Questions for Discussion

1. What do you think is the opinion of most people of faith regarding heaven?

2. The chapter looks at both the original creation in the Garden as well as the final statements at the end of the Book of Revelation and notes that "God doesn't change." What is the point being made here?

3. Popular cartoon images show heaven as a place where people wear white robes, have halos, walk on clouds and play harps. Is that a compelling image for you? What is your reaction to the chapter's suggestion that the Bible promises a "new earth" instead of heaven?

4. The chapter notes that heaven is a spiritual realm, God's "control room" as it were. It suggest that whether we are destined to go there is related to the matter of bodily resurrection. Discuss.

5. What did you think of the author's "little speculation" at the end of the chapter in which he notes that "time is our problem" not God's, and entertains the thought of all of us "arriving" in eternity at the same time? Does it answer any questions for you? Does it perhaps create other ones?

8. When All Is Said and Done
"... and What It Does"

... and What It Does. Indeed, when all is said and done, what remains and what is important is what the Bible *does* say. Christ, Cross, Resurrection, as I said at the beginning. If we have these three straight, the rest will pretty much fall into place. Yet our wrestling with things that the Bible *doesn't* say has also been fruitful. What I want to do now is pull all seven chapters together and then make some suggestions as to where this all goes.

Adam's rib. When God takes a side, instead of a rib, a point is made. Whether or not you understand Genesis 1 to say that God began by creating the *'adam"* as a single male-female creature, the poetic structure and Hebrew vocabulary still speak volumes about men and women standing together on the same rung of the ladder.

In Genesis 1:27, the phrase "male and female" is put in parallel with "image of God," showing from the get-go that women share the image of God every bit as much as men. Yet this creation of the *'adam"* is seen by God to be incomplete. "It is not good for the man to be alone" (Genesis 2:18). So God, whom the Bible again and again describes as our *'ezer* – our "helper"– creates the woman to be the *'ezer* of the Man. He does so by "splitting the *'adam"* and taking a "side" (not a "rib") to fashion the woman. Equality. Parity. Partnership. Only after the Fall in Genesis 3, when sin enters the world and the creation suffers a twist, is the woman told, "and he will rule over you."

So what *about* the Fall and its cause? What lies behind the snake which led the woman and the man to take of the forbidden fruit in order to "be like God"?

Genesis says nothing about *the fall of Satan*. Genesis 3 just speaks of a snake or a serpent – albeit one which talked. It takes a reading of the whole Bible to make the connection between that snake and Satan. Yet of Satan's origin the Bible says nothing; it remains a mystery. The popular story of a proud and beautiful angel named Lucifer mounting a rebellion and being cast out of heaven with the angels who joined him is not found. Rather, it appears to be an amalgamation of prophecies in Isaiah 14 against the king of Babylon and in Ezekiel 28 against the prince of Tyre. Yet what *of* those prophecies? They are certainly suggestive and, at times, seem to go beyond describing mere mortals.

It is left to the reader to decide whether there is, in these texts, a hint of dark and primordial satanic origins, but our study made one important thing very clear: Satan is neither a god nor is he, in some way, "equal but opposite" to God. The Bible is not dualistic, and Satan is understood to be a creature, not divine,[1] and thus ultimately answerable to God. Whatever Satan's origins, we are to take him seriously, yes, but not stand in fear of him. He is already a defeated enemy, overcome by the Cross and Resurrection of Christ. This retreating enemy can still leave chaos in his wake, but his fate is ultimately sealed and we live in the promise of resurrection and a new creation.

And there is this – a point I didn't make earlier. Although the Bible doesn't clearly mention any primordial rebellion on the part

---

[1] Remember: nowhere is it suggested that Satan is omniscient, omnipotent or omnipresent.

of Satan, it does point clearly to *another* ancient rebellion: our own. We may want to brush things off with a cute "the Devil made me do it," but the Bible suggests nothing cute about sin. The snake actually gets very little press in Genesis, but the rebellion of the man and the woman and their descendants – and God's cleaning up the mess – takes up the rest of the Bible. The knowledge of good and evil – but also the stain of original sin – is passed on from generation to generation. And the trait of knowing the good yet doing the evil finally comes even to us. Along with death.

But if death is our fate, what happened to *Eternal Life*? Turns out we didn't lose it; rather, we never had it. Because of our attempt to become like God, our propensity for knowing the good but doing the evil, and our playing God with the lives of others, the potential for eternal life was, in the end, withdrawn from us. We had gained knowledge, but the weight of that particular knowledge was too great for us to bear. It exceeded our design specs, so to speak, and, were we to live forever, there would be no end to the desolation wrought. Death, it turns out, was a mercy after all!

Yet there remained an untouched tree in the Garden: the tree of life. What was that all about? When I was a child, I sometimes wondered, "Is it still there to this day? What if we could get to it and taste of its fruit? Would it still be possible for us to live forever?"

But I was missing the point, as I so often have done. The tree of life, in Genesis 1, remains not as something for modern explorers to discover – like Ponce de León seeking the "fountain of youth" or Livingstone hunting for the headwaters of the Nile – but rather as a reminder of God's original intent for us. Yes, life eternal is something God wanted – and wants – for all of us. That's what the presence of the tree of life in Genesis[2] – and then at the very end in Revelation[3] – tells us. But, as it turns out, only God himself is now able to bring that about.

It's the puzzle of *Jesus' "descent into hell"* that makes that clear. It took Christ, the Cross and the Resurrection for eternal life to become available again. And, in chapter 4 above, it took a lot of digging through *gehenna* and Hades to make it clear that the Bible speaks not of Jesus descending to hell but rather of a descent to the dead. And why? That the Gospel might come also to those who lived before the time of Christ, in order that the will of God, "who desires all men to be saved" (1 Timothy 2:4), might be realized. In other words, the work of Christ in his Cross and Resurrection was not merely for Peter, James and John – and us – but also for Adam and Eve, Abraham and Sarah, and countless others through time and space. It is God's will that they, too, know eternal life.

But then we came to the question of what form eternal life will take. *What happens when we die?* Do we become angels? Do our "immortal souls" fly off to heaven as our decrepit bodies molder in the grave? Those very popular views are also among the many things that are not found in the Bible. Rather, the Bible speaks of something much more tangible, down to earth, intriguing and hopeful.

---

[2] Genesis 2:9; 3:22, 24.

[3] Revelation 2:7; 22:1, 2, 14, 19. The tree of life is also referenced four time in Proverbs (3:18; 11:30; 13:12; 15:4), but purely as metaphor for something good without any sense of location (such as in the Garden of Genesis 2-3 or the City of Revelation.21-22).

We were created not as ephemeral spirits or souls but rather as body-and-soul creatures. That is what God intends us to be, and the Bible says nothing about our becoming angels. The Bible also knows nothing of souls, freed from their bodies, flitting off to heaven. That spirit-vs-body idea is the stuff of Greek philosophy, not New Testament hope.

What we *do* find in the New Testament (and what is hinted at and longed for in the Old Testament) is the promise that we will, on the last day, be raised again, body and soul, finally restored to be the way God originally created us and intended us to be. And that should not be such a strange thought to us once we realize that God doesn't change and neither does his will for us.

If that be the case, however, then arises the question of *where* we shall be. Can resurrected body-and-soul creatures truly find a home in the spiritual realm of heaven? Before getting to that final question, however, we took a small detour to explore what, for some, has become an anxiety-producing cul-de-sac.

The New Testament speaks of Christ returning to gather his own. So, when that happens, ***what if you get "left behind"***? The question has, in recent years, become a burning one for many. Yet a close reading of the verses that are so often quoted raises questions about this recent popular scenario of pilotless planes crashing and driverless cars veering off of highways, leaving the carnage to be dealt with by those who are left behind. Now, indeed, we do want to be among those gathered by Christ upon his return. But, as we saw in chapter 6, when Jesus says that "one will be taken and one will be left," right after mentioning those "taken" by the flood at the time of Noah, the implication seems to be that one should indeed *want* to be "left behind."

But left behind where? ... and for what? Well, if Paul's imagery at the end of 1 Thessalonians 4 is indeed based upon the pattern of a royal visit, then those who "meet the Lord in the air" will accompany him not up to heaven but as he continues down to earth. So what about the relationship of heaven to earth and of both to our eternal destiny? That question was dealt with in the final chapter.

Where is heaven? ... and when? In the Bible, heaven is God's realm; it's the "control room," if you will. We are body-soul creatures, created with a physical environment in mind. This was most clear when God originally placed our primordial ancestors in the Garden of Eden. But it also becomes clear, as we read the New Testament closely, that God's final destiny for us is physical in nature, not spiritual – even though this rather flies in the face of contemporary popular opinion.

Jesus tells the thief on the cross that he will be with him in *paradeisos* – a word that is used, in the Greek translation of the Old Testament, to mean the Garden of Eden – a location both physical and earthbound. We are told that we have a "citizenship ... in heaven," but, in the very next words, heaven is a place "*from* which also we eagerly wait for a Savior, the Lord Jesus Christ" (Phil 3:20). Likewise, we have an inheritance "reserved for you in heaven" (1 Peter 1:4), and in the Gospels we are told that we have a "reward" or "treasure" in heaven.

Taken together, these texts seem to consider heaven to be a repository of our future blessings, much like a bank being the present holder of an inheritance we will receive at a future date. Just as we don't ever go to live in the bank, so, it would appear, our destiny is not heaven but elsewhere. But where?

The answer begins in the Old Testament. There, in Isaiah 65 and 66, God promises a "new heavens and a new earth" – a theme picked up by Peter and Paul and also by John in the book of Revelation. In Revelation 21, John sees "the holy city, new Jerusalem, coming down out of heaven from God" and hears a loud voice which proclaims, "Behold, the tabernacle [dwelling place] of God is among men, and He will dwell among them, and they shall be His people."

God's intentions for us do not change. He originally placed us, as body-soul creatures in need of a physical environment, in a garden on a newly created earth. In the end, there will be a "new earth" on which we will dwell; but this time the image is of a city instead of a garden.

Now, for Christians this is really nothing new. It's as old as the ancient Gloria Patri which you may sing, or may remembering having sung, in worship: "Glory be to the Father, and to the Son and to the Holy Ghost. As it was in the beginning, is now and ever shall be, world without end. Amen."[4] There it is again. Perhaps you've sung that many times and never noticed the way in connects the end with the beginning in terms of a "world without end."

A final thought – and a challenge. The Old Testament generally speaks of "the day of the LORD" whereas the New Testament, following the lead of Isaiah in the Old, awaits a "new heaven and a new earth." They are not the same. The Old

---

[4] The Gloria Patri goes back to the fifth or sixth century and is found in many ancient languages. The wording I use here goes back at least to the Anglican *Book of Common Prayer* edited by Thomas Cranmer in 1549 and revised in 1552.

Testament "day of the LORD" is envisioned as a day within history when God enters the world to right all wrongs, to bring justice, and to restore his suffering creation. There is historical continuity between the old and the new.

The New Testament, on the other hand, frames its expectations in a literary form known as apocalyptic. You know apocalyptic; it's the style found in the book of Revelation and in the last six chapters of Daniel, and is filled with symbolic numbers, beasts and visions. Most importantly, apocalyptic – and thus the New Testament – speaks in terms of historical *dis*continuity. The world is destroyed, not righted, and is replaced by a *new* (heavens and) earth. The two views are rather different.

The thought: what if both are really saying the same thing? What if the Bible is really consistent on this matter and both the Old and the New Testaments are in agreement on this matter? What if the apocalyptic style of the New Testament – and, in particular, of the book of Revelation – is just that: a *style*, a container for the same message as found in the Old Testament with its "day of the LORD" and its historical continuity? In other words, should we be looking not for a day of destruction of our present world but of its restoration? This would not be by our own efforts, certainly – in regard to *those* efforts I am a theological pessimist, not a humanistic optimist. Rather, it would be a final mighty act of God.

If that would be the case, then comes **the challenge:** If this world in which we live at present is, in the end, going to be restored by God, rather than destroyed, then what ought to be our attitude toward it today? Genesis tells us that, at every step in his creation of this wonderful world, God "saw that it was good."[5] Only after our rebellion, known as The Fall, did a twist enter into God's perfect creation.

Today, as a result, not everything that happens in our world is the will of God. Instead, we await the day when all will again be put right – that great hope for creation to be "set free from its bondage to decay" as we saw expressed in Romans 8. If, indeed, this is to involve a restoring of this world in which we live at present, then that implies that this world is not merely disposable, something that is "going to disappear anyway when Christ returns." And if that be the case, then how should we be treating it? Should we not still be seeking to "serve it and to preserve it" (the literal meaning of the Hebrew of Genesis 2:15)?

And what about the "when"? What about my speculation concerning eternity to the left and the thin veil through which we pass? Take that for what you will. It's certainly discussable and arguable but not essential. It is speculation, after all, and not a die-for issue like Christ, Cross and Resurrection. Because, as I said at the beginning, Christ, Cross and Resurrection is where we need to have our feet planted before we talk about anything else. That's what the Bible *does* say.

---

[5] Genesis 1:10, 12, 18, 21, 25, 31. The first time that God pronounced something "not good" was when he noted that the man was alone (Genesis 2:18).

And What Do You Say? Questions for Discussion

1. Review the summary this chapter provides of the whole book. If you are in a group, bring up and discuss some of the questions that remain for you.

2. What is the difference between the Old Testament "Day of the Lord" and the apocalyptic view found in the New Testament – and particularly in the Book of Revelation?

3. In what way does the chapter suggest they might both be saying the same thing?

4. What is being suggested in the next to last paragraph of the chapter in terms of our care of the earth?

5. Compare the first paragraph of the book's Preface to the last paragraph at the end of the book. Where does the author say our feet should be firmly planted? Do you agree or disagree? Why?

Index of Scripture

Genesis
1.27	3- 6
1-2	24
2.4	2
2.17	23
2.18	3
2.21-22	4
2.21-23	1
3	13, 20, 25, 27
5.24	18
6.1-12	11
32.1-3	42
50.19-21	28

1 Chronicles 21.1	16

Job 1-2	14-15

Psalm 24	5

Ecclesiastes 12.7	43

Isaiah
5.7	5
14.12-15	16
65.17-18	71
66.22	72

Ezekiel 28	9, 17, 18, 21

Zechariah 3	15, 16

Matthew
5.12	66
6.19-20	66
12.40	35
19.21	66
22.30	42
24.31	56
24.36-42	57
24.40-42	53, 57
24-25	56

Mark
12.18-27	45
12.25	42
13	56
13.26-27	56

Luke
10.17-18	10
10.19-20	10
16.19-31	67
17	56
17.34-36	57
20.36	42
21	56
21.27-28	57
23.42-43	67

John
5.25	35-36
8.58	76
11.23-27	45
14.2-3	69

Acts
4.1-2	46
7.59	44
17.32	46
23.6	48

| 24.21 | 48 |
| 24.25 | 48 |

Romans
1.8	69
8.11	47
8.18-23	72
10.6-7	69

1 Corinthians
6.14	47
8.5	69
15	44-45
15.47	69

2 Corinthians
4.14	47
5.1-4	70
5.1-9	47
12.2-4	67, 69

Ephesians
| 4.8-10 | 36 |
| 6.9 | 69 |

Philippians
1.23	47
3.10-11	47
3.14	70
3.20	70

Colossians
| 1.5 | 71 |
| 4.1 | 69 |

1 Thessalonians
1.10	69
4.13-18	53, 55, 58-60
4.16	46

2 Thessalonians 1.7 | 69 |

1 Peter
1.4	67
1.12	42
3.18-20	36-37
4.6	37

2 Peter
| 2.4-5 | 11 |
| 3.10-13 | 72 |

Jude 5-6 | 11 |

Revelation
2.7	67, 75
4.1	65
12.7-9	12, 13, 20
20.1-3	13, 20
21.1-4	73
22.2	26

Index of Subjects

Angels............ 9, 11-15, 18, 41-42, 44, 48, 56, 58-59, 80, 82, 83

Apocalyptic... 86

Apostles' Creed........................... 31-32, 34, 37-38, 41

Day of the LORD 85-86

Enoch 10.. 18-19

Gehenna 33-34, 37, 68

Hades 33-34

Hell...................................... 11, 31-35, 37, 82

Immortality................................. 23-26, 41-43, 48, 82

"Left Behind" Series..................................... 53-54

Lucifer................................... viii, 9, 17-18, 80

New earth 64, 71-73, 75, 77, 85

Paradise....................................... 64, 66-69, 75

Paradise Lost (John Milton) 19-20

Poetry, Hebrew.. 4-5

Rapture, The....................................... 53-58, 60

Resurrection of the dead................ 41-42, 45-46, 48, 64, 76-77

Satan 9-17, 19-21

Septuagint, the 68

Sheol.. 33-34

The Pit... 33

Tree of life 24-26, 67, 75, 81-82

Other Books by the Author:

Available on Amazon.com

Leaning into the Future: The Gospel According to the Old Testament
126 pages, 6" x 9"

"They let Jesus in, but they took away his Bible." These are the opening words of this book which contends that Christians often miss the boat when they read only the New Testament or when the Old Testament is no longer read in worship services.

The Old Testament, after all, was the Bible of the early church and was, indeed, Jesus' Bible as well as that of Peter, John, Paul, and the other followers of Christ. If you really want to understand Jesus, you need to understand his Bible. And there is more.

The Old Testament actually contains gospel – good news – of its own, starting with God declaring that all of creation is very good, to the Exodus – even to the forgotten introduction of the Ten Commandments. And then there are the darker questions of God's "jealousy," of slavery, and of the place of women, none of which turn out to be as dark as many have imagined as the Old Testament leans into the future.

You Can Understand the Old Testament
306 pages, 6" x 9"

This is a book for those who are at times puzzled or put off by the Old Testament because of simply not knowing where to begin. The book provides both introduction and overview, exploring the meaning and message of each book for readers of today.

The book begins with the sometimes contentious question of why (and whether) the Old Testament is "old,"and then moves into introductions to each of its major sections. Individual overviews and discussions of each book of the Old Testament are provided along with helpful maps, tables and charts as well as complete indexes of subject matter, biblical texts cited, and Hebrew words noted in the discussion.

The book is written for students of the Bible, whether members of church congregations, pastors, or students in college or seminary. No knowledge of Hebrew is assumed or required; but, for those who have studied that language, the book offers additional insights based on the Hebrew text. The first edition of the book was published for classroom use by the author, who taught Old Testament and Hebrew in seminary for 13 years. This second edition has been revised with the audience described above in mind.

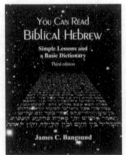

You Can Read Biblical Hebrew
338 pages, 8.5" x 11"

Yes, you *can*, indeed, learn to read Biblical Hebrew.

Although the lessons are simple, the content is complete and covers all aspects of classical Biblical Hebrew.

The text is suitable for self-study or classroom use and its 78 lessons cover two semesters worth of material. The large format leaves room for personal notes and contains exercises with keys, self-test check boxes within the text, complete verb tables, a detailed Hebrew-English lexicon (dictionary), as well as an Index of Hebrew words discussed within the text and a Subject Index.

Earlier editions were used for 13 years in classroom teaching as well as by individuals for self-study. When you complete the lessons and exercises of this book, you *will* be able to read Biblical Hebrew.

Sidelined but Not Abandoned: The Fate of the Firstborn in Genesis
308 pages, 6" x 9"

Was Cain treated unfairly by God? What does it mean that God would not give Ishmael the Abrahamic covenant and yet promised to "make him fruitful and multiply him" such that he would become "the father of twelve princes, and ... a great nation" even before such things were promised to Jacob? Would you rather have

Jacob or Esau as your next door neighbor? Read the text carefully before you answer, and you may be surprised at your conclusion. Was it lust or arrogance that led to Reuben's downfall?

All these were firstborn; all were kicked to the side of the road by God. Or were they? What was actually happening in these Genesis encounters with destiny? In what sense were the firstborn in Genesis "sidelined but not abandoned"?

This book, originally the author's Ph.D. thesis, is being published for two reasons. The first is to make the basic research available more widely, since some of the observations are critical and yet have not been widely noted. The other reason: after more than two decades of reflection as a seminary professor and pastor, the author has concluded that the "sidelining" of the firstborn in Genesis is part of a larger picture that, ultimately, reveals the intent of the entire book.

Edited by the Author:
Available on Amazon.com

The Traditional Musical Instruments of Tanzania
86 pages, 6" x 9"

This book is a slight revision of the original 1990 edition, originally published in Dar es Salaam, Tanzania. Compiled by Gareth W. Lewis and E. G. Makala, with illustrations by J. Masanja, this work organizes and presents the traditional musical instruments of Tanzania according to four categories familiar to musicologists:

(1) Idiophones
(2) Membranophones (drums)
(3) Aerophones and
(4) Chordophones.

In each case, instruments are discussed according to Typical names, Geographic locations, Description and mode of manufacture, Manner of playing, Uses and other remarks.

A primary concern is to preserve the ethnic musical heritage of Tanzania in an age in which traditional music is being displaced, if not obliterated, by the continued encroachments of western electronic music. In the closing words of Lewis' introduction: "If Tanzania is losing its traditional music, then at least there is a record of the musical instruments available. And perhaps this work will spur people to record a complex and often beautiful musical culture and perhaps to act to reverse its decline."

CPSIA information can be obtained
at www.ICGtesting.com
Printed in the USA
LVHW04s0207180918
590501LV00010B/221/P